NOT ROCKET SURGERY

An Employer's Guide to Controlling the Health Care Supply Chain

Mike Hill, RHU, REBC, LIC

Copyright © 2018 by Michael Hill. All rights reserved. Printed in the United States of America. No part of this book may be used or reproduced in any manner whatsoever without written permission.

Printed in the United States of America
10 9 8 7 6 5 4 3 2 1

Library of Congress Cataloging-in-Publication Data is available for this title.

Editing and Proofreading by Ingrid Benson
Cover design by Rachel Ozios
Text design and composition by Macatawa Publishing Services
Printed by CreateSpace, An Amazon.com Company

Distributed by Amazon

Contents

Foreword	4
Introduction	7
About the Author	8
Dedication	9
Chapter 1 Introduction: There Is Profit in Health Insurance	10
Chapter 2 Employers Haven't Had Control	15
Chapter 3 What Is a Total Control Health Plan?	22
Chapter 4 Management	31
Chapter 5 Access to Information	47
Chapter 6 Access to Providers	65
Chapter 7 Pharmacy Benefit Managers	90
Chapter 8 Innovation	111
Chapter 9 Auto Adjudication	119
Chapter 10 Brokers Haven't Influenced Price	125
Chapter 11 What I Haven't Talked About…Yet	140
Chapter 12 Complacency	146
Appendix NextGen Benefits Mastermind Partners Member List	151

Foreword
By Mat Nguyen
President of Worksighted, Inc.

When we founded our company in 2000, my partner and I had a vision to create a unique business that brought enterprise level IT services and support to the small- and medium-sized business market. While many said it couldn't be done, we firmly believed it could and we set out to prove the naysayers wrong. We were entrepreneurs in the truest sense of the word, continuously investing every asset we had in the business to achieve our dream of building something that was unique in the marketplace, both in terms of the services we provide to our customers and the internal culture that allows us to continue reinventing ourselves.

Now, 17 years and 80 employees later, we still live by the same entrepreneurial approach to everything that we do and it has served our company well. By taking a fresh, never been done before approach, our team has been able to find new and innovative ways to serve our customers, while at the same time identify and partner with similarly-minded vendor partners and leaders who have made our company better. Many of the vendor partners we use have been with us from the beginning, and with few exceptions the services we receive today are better than when we started working together, and in many cases the costs have come down. At the end of each year, we reflect on the past 12 months and it has always been clear that our company has grown and evolved and continues to move in a positive direction. From multiple moves to bigger and better office space, to additional employee benefits such as flexible work environments, we have been able to differentiate our business by being uniquely different from our competition.

The lone standout, however, is what we've experienced with our health insurance. While we have sought out innovative ways to offer our employees high quality and affordable health insurance options, the market simply hasn't had any to offer. As early adopters of high deductible health plans with Health Savings Accounts, we were hopeful that our willingness to engage our employees in meaningful conversations about their role in containing health care costs would be rewarded with lower, or at least stable, costs. The unfortunate reality, however, has been that health insurance is the only item in our benefit program that has gotten massively more expensive over the last 15 years and as a result, the plans we are able to offer our employees have gotten worse while at the same time our employees now pay more than before.

As with any company, health insurance is incredibly important to both my partner and me for personal reasons. Over the last 17 years, we have explored many different opportunities to reduce the cost of our health insurance while at the same time offering high quality coverage to our colleagues. What we have found is that there are two distinct realities in the employer health insurance market. (1) Enterprise level employers with tens of thousands or hundreds of thousands of employees have been able to benefit from unique and everchanging strategies such as direct contracting, bulk purchasing, medical tourism, and others. (2) At the same time, small- and medium-sized businesses have consistently been told that it isn't for them; they are simply too small to use these same strategies so we've been left to accept paying more and getting less as our only reality. This message struck me as one very similar to what my partner and I were told when we wanted to bring enterprise level IT solutions to the small- and medium-sized business market.

It is for this reason, as both a business owner and participant in my company's health insurance plan, that I am so excited about the concept of the Total Control Health Plan, which is the first meaningful innovation in the health insurance space that I've seen since we started our business. The TCHP model has given us the ability to use the same entrepreneurial, strategic management practices we have used in all the other aspects of our business and as a result, we are now in the position to implement a health plan that aligns with our culture and values. The Total Control Health Plan gives us the ability to use the same strategies that employers like Walmart have been using for years to keep their costs manageable while at the same time enhancing the quality of their coverage.

I commend Mike Hill for not taking "no" for an answer and setting out to help employers address an issue that has reached the level of full-blown crisis. We are now in a position to use the same entrepreneurial start-up mentality on one of our biggest line items—to address an unsustainable issue.

Introduction

While health insurance can be very intimidating and seemingly complex, when broken down to the component parts, it becomes clear that the opposite is actually true. Like all other types of insurance, health insurance is simply a mechanism for transferring risk from one party to another, and in the case of health insurance, the risk is the financial liability of health care costs.

If health insurance is actually relatively simple, why then has a meaningful solution to address the rising cost of health insurance been so hard to identify? In reality, a solution does exist and it has been right in front of us for years. While many will argue otherwise, the solution to rising health care and health insurance costs isn't complicated like brain surgery or rocket science. Simply put, fixing the rising cost of health insurance is Not Rocket Surgery, and any employer who elects to do so can reduce the cost of their corporate health insurance program dramatically and permanently. The solution is the Total Control Health Plan.

About the Author

Mike Hill has been advising employers on health care cost reduction strategies for nearly two decades. An expert in self-funded medical plans, Mike has helped employers implement varied solutions focused on controlling cost drivers and reducing the cost of health care, such as direct contracting, direct primary care, and others, as a means to return the crown jewel of employee benefit packages to its place of prominence rather than the liability that it has become.

Understanding that pre-packed fully insured medical plans eliminate all employer control over their health care supply chain, Mike wrote *Not Rocket Surgery, An Employer's Guide to Controlling the Health Care Supply Chain*, which introduces the concept of the Total Control Health Plan. Mike is passionate about putting employers in a position to use the same techniques they use to manage all other aspects of their business on their health plans. By doing so, employers have not only experienced dramatic cost reductions and flat annual increases, but they have done so while providing better plans to their employees.

Mike is a member of the NextGen Benefits Mastermind Partnership, and serves and has served his community as a Board member of multiple non-profit organizations.

Dedication

This book is dedicated to my incredibly supportive wife, Colleen, and to all of the talented professionals who have shared words of wisdom and invested in me and my career.

Chapter 1
Introduction: There Is Profit in Health Insurance

At the 2017 Berkshire Hathaway shareholders' meeting, Warren Buffet stated, "Medical costs are the tapeworm of American economic competitiveness." The statement was made as part of a broader conversation, where Mr. Buffett was arguing that business leaders have been focused on issues like reducing taxes while ignoring the giant shop vac of business profits, corporate health insurance.

According to the opensecrets.org lobbying database, the health sector, which includes pharmaceuticals/ health products, hospitals/nursing homes, health professionals, health services/HMOs, and miscellaneous health (in other words, the health care supply chain), is in the top three sectors in terms of dollars spent on lobbying each year going as far back as 1998. In the year 2000, the health sector was third, spending $208,201,150. In 2016 and 2017, the health sector was number one, spending $555,010,000 on lobbying. As the fourth-ranked industry in terms of percentage of GDP in the US, it isn't too surprising to see that industry ranked near the top from a lobbying standpoint as well.[1]

I understand the need to advocate on behalf of your industry as things can change dramatically with the stroke of the pen. That being said, of the $555,010,000 spent on lobbying, how much was spent advocating for a disruption of the status quo? How much was spent advocating for lower insurance premiums for employers and

---

[1] https://www.opensecrets.org/lobby/top.php?indexType=c&showYear=2018, accessed June 2018.

their employees? I would argue none of it, as all of the players within the health care supply chain have a vested interest in maintaining the status quo. Put another way, billions of dollars have been spent by the health sector lobbying over the last 20 years, however, the cost for health care and therefore health insurance, has done nothing but increase year over year.

Health care represents 8% of US GDP and per capita health care spending in the US is the highest in the world at $9,237 while ranking 12th in life expectancy among the 12 wealthiest industrialized countries according to the Kaiser Family Foundation. Compare that to the UK, which spends $3,749 per capita and has a higher average life expectancy. Clearly it isn't a matter of throwing enough money at it, because we've been doing that for many years and it hasn't worked. Additionally, there is almost universal consensus that the path we, as a country, are on is unsustainable, however, at the same time the health sector is spending over half a billion dollars per year advocating to maintain the status quo for one simple reason—because it works for them.

The problem with the status quo, is that it is based on misaligned incentives where in order for the insurance carriers, pharmacies, hospitals, doctors, pharmaceutical manufacturers, durable medical equipment providers, and insurance consultants to win, it seems employers need to lose. As this book will argue, by rejecting the status quo and taking a fresh look at employer-sponsored health insurance, it is possible to eliminate misaligned incentives so that every player in the system is benefiting from the exchange. By doing so, employers will find that what was once a forgone conclusion of perpetually increasing health insurance costs will change.

This book is targeted toward business owners, CEOs, CFOs, or anyone else responsible for managing the profit and loss of their respective business. If employer-sponsored health insurance was a mountain range, I'm here to tell you that there is gold in them there hills.

The purpose of this book is not to argue for a single-payer system, or to outline strategies to get out of the health insurance business. With the current administration in the White House and the employer mandate remaining intact, in addition to many other reasons, I don't believe employer-sponsored health insurance is going anywhere anytime soon. This book is meant to arm business leaders with headlamps and pick axes so that they can start mining their respective plans for gold. Not only that, but it will also outline how health insurance can regain its place as a positive employee benefit that sets employers apart from their competition.

Throughout my career working with employers to set up and maintain employee benefits, the status quo in dealing with rising health care costs has been to find creative ways to deflect the annual cost increases. Employers have been in a defensive posture rather than an offensive one. Rarely would my clients and their employees come away from the annual renewal process feeling good about the direction things were heading. The best case would be that nothing changed from one year to the next, but things certainly didn't get better. When meeting with employees, the first two questions I'd get were, "How much more is this going to cost me?" and "What did you do to my plan?" This is no way to live. Employers regularly tell me their benefit program is a key component of their attraction and retention strategy, while at the same time the most visible piece of it got progressively more expensive and worse at the same time. Something that was intended to be a positive differentiating factor is quickly becoming the opposite and is starting to limit an employer's ability to attract and retain employees.

With the rate at which employee payroll contributions are increasing far exceeding the rate of inflation, as well as wage increases, many employees are going backward from an income standpoint with health insurance being the cause. With affordable housing being a big issue in many parts of the country and other necessities such as daycare getting more expensive, employees are already starting to balk at the idea of seeing more and more of their income go to health insurance premiums.

Employers are in a tough spot because they are legally obligated to offer health insurance to their employees as the result of the Affordable Care Act, while at the same time it continues to get more and more expensive and they have been presented few options to effectively deal with the rising costs. Each year employers shop around for the same or better coverage at a lower cost, but rarely has this been an effective long-term strategy. Short of finding a better deal from another carrier, employers have been left with absorbing the cost, passing it to employees, reducing benefits, or a combination of all three.

The issue is that one of the primary tools employers have used to reduce costs is going to start vanishing for more and more employers very soon. With the Affordable Care Act setting a maximum out-of-pocket dollar amount that a compliant plan can have, employers are starting to find themselves running out of ways to reduce benefits to keep costs down. Many employers are increasing deductibles to the point that they nearly align with the total out-of-pocket. While the maximum out-of-pocket increases slightly each year, it isn't nearly enough to address the increases in premiums each year. Once an employer's plan deductible bumps up against the maximum out-of-pocket, the only traditional options left to the employer will be to absorb future increases or pass more costs along to employees. As covered above, this will turn what is supposed to be a key benefit into a massive liability.

It doesn't have to be this way. If your health insurance plan and the strategies you've been using to manage it are working for you, then this book isn't for you. If, however, you could use additional profit while at the same time offering a higher quality health insurance plan to your employees, then keep reading. Generally speaking, transactions that take place within a free market are a win-win for both parties involved. The party selling the product or service receives what they feel is a fair price and the consumer receives a product or service at a price they are comfortable with. Unfortunately, none of the forces at work in a typical market exist in the health care market, making it a very one-sided transaction and employers have largely footed the bill. It is time the tables are turned and employers take control over their plans so that they have an equal footing in the transaction. By implementing a Total Control Health Plan, employers can take an offensive posture and reverse the trend of steadily increasing costs. This book will walk you through what a Total Control Health Plan is and what implementing one would mean for your employees and your bottom line.

Chapter 2
Employers Haven't Had Control

The highlight of my career has been working with business leaders. I absolutely love working with entrepreneurs and having a peek behind the curtain of what they have built. While each story is very much unique, there have been common themes I've seen from business to business. Successful business leaders are constantly thinking about the future, taking risks, innovating, and reinventing their businesses. No businesses today are using the same computers they once had. What I've realized, though, is that there is one very important cost center in each business that hasn't evolved or seen any risk taking or innovation, and frankly, it hasn't had effective management either. That area is health insurance, the cornerstone of any employee benefit package.

I make this statement, not as an indictment of those running the business, but rather to point out that most employers have found themselves in a position where they can't meaningfully impact one of the largest expenses most businesses face. Simply put, over the last 30 or more years, most employers have been along for the ride as their health care costs have gone up year over year. It certainly isn't something that they've been happy about, but employers have been conditioned to feel good about getting something that is less bad than it could have been each year. It is very much like the fable about the frog being boiled alive. Each year the temperature is ratcheted up slightly in the form of higher premiums/costs, and the strategies that have been used to address the rising water temperature don't really do anything of the sort.

Employers may have thought they had control over their plan and the direction it was headed in when they selected things like:

- Which plan to offer
- Which carrier to work with
- How much to charge their employees
- Which advisor to work with

In reality, employers haven't had any control at all. The fact is, the health care and health insurance industries have evolved over time to the reality we face today where everyone simply accepts that costs get more expensive each year. This isn't to say that employers and their employees like it, but the vast majority of employers are resigned to the fact that they can't effectively control their health insurance costs. The current structure of the health care supply chain, built on a lack of transparency, leaves employers completely in the dark as to who is getting paid what and why. The traditional health insurance transaction does not contain the key component of an efficient market where both sides have equal access to the same information and can therefore make decisions based on value.

In his 2010 book, *The Company That Solved Health Care*, John Torinus, Jr. chronicles the steps his business, Serigraph (a company located in Wisconsin with approximately 1200 lives covered), took to address their skyrocketing costs starting in 2004. John had the following to say about the way businesses have approached health care, "Lastly, I would like to make a class-action apology for all CEOs. We allowed the mess on the economic side of health care to happen. We did not use the "Golden Rule" — he who has gold rules. We are the payers, and we let loose the beast of hyper-inflation in health care. We did not trust and empower people to help. We did not put incentives and disincentives into place. We did not create a marketplace, the best form of price discipline. In the absence of strong leadership from business, we defaulted to government to take the lead on pricing policies and procedures."[2]

The question this then raises is, why? Why is it that employers accept a reality in which all of the strategies they use successfully throughout other aspects of the business can't be applied to their health care business (i.e., their health insurance plan)? The reason is that the health care and health insurance industries are massive feedback loops reinforcing the idea that health care gets more expensive each year and therefore health insurance needs to get more expensive each year. It's just the way it is, and there is nothing an employer can do about it—and I was part of the problem.

After 18 years in the employee benefits industry and having built a successful and growing agency based largely on traditional principles, I reached a point that something had to give. As much as I enjoyed working with our clients, I found that justifying the unjustifiable was exhausting. While we regularly presented our clients with unique strategies to mitigate their rising health insurance costs, ultimately they were all based on some version of the status quo and I'd grown tired of it. Selling a product that you have no control over and that people need but really don't like is draining. Whether it was the fact that I was turning 40 or that I just needed a fresh perspective, I set out in search of a better way and I came across a group of individuals who felt the same way that I did—the NextGen Benefits Mastermind Partnership.

The NextGen Benefits Mastermind Partnership is a network of approximately 40 independent employee benefit advisors around the country who are committed to disrupting the status quo simply because it no longer works for our clients. As a group, we meet

---

[2] John Torinus, Jr., *The Company That Solved Health Care*, (Dallas, Texas: BenBella Books, 2010), 18.

quarterly around the country to discuss the strategies and vendor partners that are delivering results in changing the status quo and returning hard-earned profit to our clients. It was with input from these industry thought leaders that the concept of the Total Control Health Plan was born as a new way to view employer-sponsored health insurance. Those of us in the NextGen Benefits Mastermind Partnership are not alone either. More and more employers, along with their employees, are starting to say "enough" with the status quo.

On Tuesday, January 30, 2018, all of the large commercial insurance carriers saw massive drops in their stock price when markets opened. The reason? Amazon, Berkshire Hathaway, and JP Morgan announced they'd had enough and were creating a new health care company that eliminates the misaligned incentives that are pervasive throughout health care today, and to reduce the cost of health care for their 500,000 employees. While the most recent example of employers taking matters into their own hands, it certainly isn't the only example. In 2016, over three dozen of the country's largest employers came together to form the Health Transformation Alliance with their one stated goal to be to "fix our broken health care system." All of these employers have one thing in common, they've said "enough!" There is good news for anyone reading this book, you don't have to be a Fortune 500 company to change your health care trajectory.

Certainly, there have been "strategies" employers have used to mitigate the impact of increases each year, but when I dissect some of the most popular strategies currently used, you will realize that none of them have had or will have a meaningful impact on cost long term. The current health care supply chain is filled with smart and savvy businesses who have been thriving. They haven't been acting in a malicious way, but rather doing the same things all businesses do: work to exploit the market they function in for the financial gain of their shareholders. The issue is that all of this has happened at the expense of those footing the bill and in the US the bill is largely paid for by insurance. Forty-nine percent of all Americans get their insurance from an employer-sponsored plan, and therefore employers have been the primary source of income for all players in the health care supply chain.

I have become convinced that if an employer truly takes control, it is absolutely possible to reduce the cost of health insurance without reducing benefits or shifting costs to employees. This is based on a few key principles:

1. While I say this a little tongue in cheek, the point this next statement makes is key to the solution. When someone asks, why is health insurance expensive? The common answer they get is that health care is expensive. Well duh, thanks for that. The point, however, is that if anything is going to be done about the cost of health insurance, then something needs to be done about the cost of health care.
2. So then, who is going to do that? It is my belief, which will be supported throughout this book, that employers and the plans they offer are ground zero for the revolution to come. Why is this? When you review all aspects of the health care supply chain, you quickly realize that the only players without a vested interest in costs continuing to rise are the rate payers and the end users. Unfortunately, the end users simply don't have the information, leverage, and often the motivation necessary to have a meaningful impact on cost, and therefore it falls to the rate payers. In the US, 49% of the population receives their insurance coverage through their employer (i.e., the rate payer), and therefore it falls to them to take on the status quo.
3. For an employer to effectively take on the status quo and achieve a favorable outcome, they must be able to use the same strategies and techniques they use for all other aspects of their business. To do this, an employer must have control over their

health insurance plan and today the vast majority of employers don't. An employer must change their mindset and implement a Total Control Health Plan (TCHP), and if they do, they will stop the price escalator they have been on.

The fact is that change is already in the works at a high rate of speed, and it is highly likely that insurance companies as we know them today are likely going to look very different 10 years from now. According to the Atlantic Information Services directory of health plans, by 2016 52% of health insurance plans on the market were owned by health systems. The health care supply chain is being vertically integrated very quickly with health insurance carriers buying health care providers and vice versa in an effort to take advantage of every opportunity to draw on efficiencies to increase their profitability. The press releases will most definitely point to lowering health care costs as the primary motivation, but don't fall for the spin. Consolidation throughout the supply chain is not new and I'm not sure about you, but I haven't seen health insurance costs go down.

From a business perspective, there are two distinct advantages for hospitals/health systems to own their own insurance company.

First, through plan design an insurance company can steer patients to their own providers by building in a higher level of benefit for services rendered at their facility. This approach enables the health system to keep what might otherwise be a relatively mobile patient in a competitive market, locked in to their providers.
Second, many hospitals/health systems will continue to benefit from the perpetuation of the existing health insurance model. The reason for this is that the existing model allows hospitals to set prices at whatever level they choose, which are then masked by confidential proprietary agreements with the health insurance carrier. This arrangement largely masks the actual cost of the

services rendered from the plan participant, reducing the likelihood of consumer resistance.

Finally, Americans have largely been conditioned to expect health insurance to get more and more expensive each year, allowing prices to ratchet up year over year unchallenged.

On the other hand, according to a June 2017 report by the Robert Wood Johnson Foundation, "since 2010, of the 37 new health insurance companies and five acquired health plans, only four were profitable in 2015, five have gone out of business, and two are in the process of being sold."[3] Certainly the jury is still out as to whether hospitals can run profitable health insurance companies and vice versa. The fact is, that regardless of whether insurance companies as we know them today exist 10 years from now, or hospitals become the new insurers, neither of those models put employers in control and therefore employer costs will continue to rise. The leadership of hospitals and insurance companies are doing the exact same things that you would do if you were leading them, seeking to thrive in a competitive and ever evolving industry. They have shown themselves to be very nimble and willing to regularly reinvent themselves, however one factor that has seemingly remained unchanged and exerted no pressure on them to change is employer-funded group health insurance. The time has come for employers to get a seat at the table and to do so they must rethink how they approach health insurance.

---

[3] Allan Baumgarten, *Analysis of Integrated Delivery Systems and New Provider-Sponsored Health Plans,* (Robert Wood Johnson Foundation, June 1, 2017), accessed April 15, 2018:
https://www.rwjf.org/en/library/research/2017/06/analysis-of-integrated-delivery-systems-and-new-provider-sponsor.html.

Chapter 3
What Is a Total Control Health Plan?

Now that we have affirmed that there is an unsustainable problem with health care costs rising unchecked for the last 30 plus years and that with few exceptions employers have been helpless to do anything about it, the remainder of this book will outline a solution. One of the most commonly repeated terms used to justify an annual increase in health care costs is "trend." Here is how PWC defines the term in their annual Medical Cost Trend projection of future health care costs:

> Medical cost trend is the projected percentage increase in the cost to treat patients from one year to the next, assuming that benefits remain the same. While it can be defined in several ways, this report estimates the projected increase in per capita costs of medical services that affect commercial insurers and large, self-insured businesses. Insurance companies use the projection to calculate health plan premiums for the coming year. For example, a 10 percent trend means that a plan that costs $10,000 per employee this year would cost $11,000 next year. The cost trend, or growth rate, is influenced primarily by:
> - Changes in the price of medical products and services, known as unit cost inflation
> - Changes in the number or intensity of services used, or changes in per capita utilization[4]

---

[4] PwC, Health Research Institute, "Medical Cost Trend: Behind the Numbers 2018," (PwC Health) 4, accessed April 15, 2018:
https://www.pwc.com/co/es/salud/publicaciones/hri-behind-the-numbers-2018.pdf.

What employers, and those who advise them, have been conditioned to believe is that anything below trend is a win. I'm here to argue, however, that employers who elect to take control over their health care plan cannot only beat the trend, but reverse it. To do so, an employer needs to put themselves in a position of control over all aspects of their health insurance plan, and the only practical way of doing so is to have a self-insured plan. As this book will outline, an employer must be able to pull every lever possible related to plan management, and they need solid information to support the decisions they make. With a fully-insured arrangement, employers either lack the ability to pull meaningful levers related to plan management, the information to effectively do so, or both.

To establish a solid foundation, I will define the terms **fully-insured** and **self-insured** so that we are all on the same page.

Fully-Insured Plan

According to the Bureau of Labor Statistics, fully-insured plan is defined as, "A plan where the employer contracts with another organization to assume financial responsibility for the enrollees' medical claims and for all incurred administrative costs."[5] Put another way, with a fully-insured plan an employer pays a monthly premium (commonly in a single, double, family, or per person on the plan format) to an insurance carrier. In return, the carrier pays the medical and prescription claims as they are incurred.

Like everything in life, there are pros and cons to the fully-insured model.
Pros:
- Predictability and ability to budget
- Outsourcing of risk to a third party

---

[5] Bureau of Labor Statistics, "Definitions of Health Insurance Terms," 2, accessed April 15, 2018: https://www.bls.gov/ncs/ebs/sp/healthterms.pdf.

- Convenience

Cons:
- Limitations on ability to customize the plan(s)
- Lack of information related to how the plan is performing and why
- Lack of levers to pull to influence price

Self-Insured Plan

A self-insured plan can take many different shapes and therefore is harder to assign a simple definition to it. That being said, there are common themes within self-insured plans and according to the BLS, a self-insured plan is, "A plan offered by employers who directly assume the major cost of health insurance for their employees. Some self-insured plans bear the entire risk. Other self-insured employers insure against large claims by purchasing stop-loss coverage. Some self-insured employers contract with insurance carriers or third party administrators for claims processing and other administrative services; other self-insured plans are self-administered. All types of plans (Conventional Indemnity, PPO, EPO, HMO, POS, and PHOs) can be financed on a self-insured basis."[6]

Pros:
- Ability to customize plan(s)
- Greater level of information related to how the plan is performing and why
- Significantly more levers to pull not only to address price of administration and stop loss but also overall plan cost

Cons:
- Depending on structure, potentially a significantly greater level of financial variability from month to month

---

[6] Bureau of Labor Statistics, "Definitions of Health Insurance Terms," 6, accessed April 15, 2018: https://www.bls.gov/ncs/ebs/sp/healthterms.pdf.

- The potential for plan performance to result in greater monthly or annual costs than a comparable fully-insured plan
- Greater level of employer engagement required to effectively manage the plan

With the basics out of the way, some readers may be contemplating putting the book down due to the fact that they have always been fully-insured and believe that it is their only practical option. Before you do, let me dispel some myths surrounding a self-insured plan and who can realistically have one.

The most commonly-used threshold for determining if self-insured is practical for an employer is group size. Depending on who you ask and where they are located, you are likely to get different answers to this question, but historically throughout the Midwest the answer has been employers with 100 employees or more. In the Southeast however, it is common to find employers with 1000+ employees who are fully-insured. While in my view 100 is a good rule of thumb, I've worked with employers who have had 30 employees and been self-insured, and those well over 300 who have been fully-insured.

So what is it about employer size that determines whether self-insuring is a reality for an employer or not? It can be boiled down to one word, "predictability" or to use an insurance term "creditability." The reality is the smaller an employer group, the more likely one particular individual could expose the plan to a disproportionate amount of risk resulting in a situation where the self-insured plan costs the employer more than they would have spent had they simply implemented a fully-insured plan. That being said, as outlined earlier in this section, there are multiple ways to design and implement a plan that would fall under the self-insured umbrella and there are many effective strategies to reduce the risk associated with the unpredictability of a smaller self-insured plan.

As outlined in Figure 3.1, health insurance plans fall on a spectrum ranging from fully-insured with little or no control to a self-insured Total Control Health Plan with ultimate control. As an employer progresses along the spectrum, they have the opportunity to gain more and more control, and also realize the fruits of their efforts in managing their plan. For the purposes of determining if you should read further, I believe most employers with 30 employees or more on their health insurance plan who desire to disrupt the status quo can absolutely leverage the concepts in this book to achieve a Total Control Health Plan.

Figure 3.1

Health Care Supply Chain

The final foundational concept required to effectively define a Total Control Health Plan is that of the health care supply chain. Thousands of books have been written about supply chain management, and any successful business leader knows that this is a key principle to business success or failure. What few businesses have realized, however, is that if they have an employer-sponsored health insurance plan, they also have a health care supply chain. From doctors and hospitals to pharmaceutical manufacturers and insurance companies, there are many different players in the health care supply chain that all contribute to the cost of health insurance.

In their 2018 predictions in the Medical Cost Trend report, PWC said the following, "For medical cost trend to sink lower than its 'new normal,' health organizations and businesses will have to consider tackling the price of services as well as the rate of utilization. Heading into 2018, employers should look to new contract arrangements with providers to tackle healthcare prices without shifting more costs to employees."[7]

To effectively do so, like every other supply chain they manage, an employer needs to dissect their health insurance plan to the individual components of the health care supply chain and implement effective strategies to manage each one. The remainder of this book will do that, but let's first identify a few key components of the health care supply chain and understand why an employer ultimately needs a self-insured plan to manage each one.

In addition to the previously stated components of the health care supply chain, the following items can be added to the list:

---

[7] PwC, Health Research Institute, "Medical Cost Trend: Behind the Numbers 2018," (PwC Health), accessed April 15, 2018:
https://www.pwc.com/co/es/salud/publicaciones/hri-behind-the-numbers-2018.pdf.

- Outpatient facilities
- Pharmacy benefit managers
- Prescription wholesalers
- Durable medical equipment manufacturers
- Durable medical equipment distributors
- Insurance carriers
- Plan administrators
- Rate payers (employers in this case)
- Consumers/patients

With so many diverse players throughout the health care supply chain, it is highly likely that diverse and unique strategies will be required to ensure the most effective management. It is also highly likely that the diverse populations from employer to employer may require different strategies for each one to best manage their health care supply chain.

If you agree with the statements I've just made, then the conclusion you will quickly reach when thinking about fully-insured medical plans is that their biggest selling point of providing a prepackaged solution to employers for a predictable cost each month is also their biggest weakness.

With fully-insured plans, an employer outsources management of their health care supply chain to an insurance carrier who uses a one size fits all approach to manage the plan to best meet the needs of the carrier. Carriers may argue that they are using the best strategies available because they are spending their money and need to manage it very wisely. While there is some truth to this, the bigger reality is that so long as the carrier establishes actuarially sound rates, any costs realized due to ineffective management of the health care supply chain are simply passed along to the rate payers.

Unfortunately, the concepts of remaining fully insured and implementing a Total Control Health Plan are mutually exclusive. You simply can't have both at the same time. This isn't to say that there isn't a need for fully-insured plans and that the carriers who offer them are doing the wrong thing. The exact opposite is true. The vast majority of fully-insured carriers throughout the country provide a much needed service and do a great job. The fact remains, however, that fully-insured premiums continue to rise year after year with no end in sight. If you, as an employer, are interested in achieving a different result, then as the saying goes, "you can't keep doing what you've always done."

If you are interested in implementing a TCHP, then you must start with selecting an independent third party administrator (TPA) to be the nucleus of your health care supply chain management strategy. The reason that it must be an independent TPA rather than a commercial carrier is that with limited exceptions the strategies they use to manage the supply chain for their fully-insured clients are the same strategies you will get with your self-insured plan. As previously stated, the definition of a TCHP will vary from employer to employer with different solutions being used for different problems from plan to plan.

I recently bought a car and arrived at the dealership with financing already lined up. To see the look on the salesperson's face when I explained this was very telling. They shortly got up and a few minutes later I was joined by the finance person who tried to persuade me to go through one of their preferred financing options instead of the option I lined up. They shared with me that they are compensated by their preferred options based on the size of their book of business with each lender. I appreciated their transparency and since they were able to match the deal I had lined up, I elected to use one of their preferred options. While I don't know how meaningful the impact was to the dealership, I am confident it was far greater than the $100 they threw my way.

The same thing happens with commercial carriers, but there is even less transparency. There are many moving pieces within a health insurance plan, many of which are provided by different entities. Commercial carriers form partnerships with various service providers who do an adequate job, but there is also likely something in it for the carriers too. While the various service providers do a fine job for the plan as a whole, it is likely that with a little digging you will find alternate options that are far more beneficial to your plan than what is being offered in the packaged solution.

Additionally, it is really hard to know exactly who is getting what and why in a repacked offering. The bundled pricing option is a common tactic used in sales to give the buyer the impression they are getting a great deal, but in reality the seller is getting the better deal. If a commercial carrier is willing to allow you to interchange various components to better manage your supply chain, then absolutely do so. It is likely, however, that simply due to the carrier business model it will be more difficult to implement new strategies to address your health care supply chain challenges. Frankly, insurance carriers have a vested interest in maintaining the status quo and their business models don't allow for innovation and disruption.

So to recap, a Total Control Health Plan is a plan that:
- Is self-insured or is progressing toward a self-insured model
- Is ultimately built around the administration by an independent TPA, or a carrier that provides complete transparency in every aspect of the plan finances and flexibility in terms of vendor partners used (Note: these are hard to find)
- Is one where an employer has the ability to effectively manage every aspect of their health care supply chain

Chapter 4
Management

Besides the funding arrangement already covered, the biggest differentiating factor between a TCHP and a typical insurance plan is the degree to which the plan is managed. With a typical plan, all the various components are lumped together in a nice turn-key package. In many cases, this is very appealing to an employer largely due to the convenience and the fact that they didn't go into business to manage health insurance plans. That being said, in order to effectively contain costs, an employer needs to be willing to deconstruct their plan to implement proven management strategies for each aspect of their health care supply chain.

An analogy I like to use to illustrate the difference between a TCHP and a traditional plan is that of an office. A traditional insurance plan is the equivalent of leasing an office that comes complete with internet, office furniture, computers, coffee, copiers, payroll services, and office supplies all wrapped up with a nice monthly payment. It certainly is convenient. The issue is, the rent gets more and more expensive every year. Additionally, you might find that the computers you are provided are pretty old and inefficient; the payroll system can't handle your unique payroll frequency; and the office furniture doesn't support your collaborative culture. At some point, it is likely that you would like to take a step back and go in search of a completely empty office that you could outfit yourself. You'd then go in search of the office furniture that fit your budget and needs, and on and on you would go until you had a better solution that was likely less expensive than what you were paying before.

The same concept applies to a Total Control Health Plan. There certainly are many instances when implementing a fully-insured plan, or a self-insured plan with a carrier makes sense. For any number of reasons, an employer may determine that the package deal is the best deal for them. The only thing to remember is that if you want to achieve different results with your health insurance plan, you need to be able to answer questions like these:

- How much am I paying for each medical claim?
- Where are the rebates going from each prescription claim, and how much are they?
- Who is helping plan participants to identify the most cost effective and high quality service providers?
- What percentage of claims submitted to my plan had errors?
- What percentage of claims submitted to my plan were unnecessary?

Of all the concepts discussed throughout this book, the concept of managing the plan is likely the most unnerving to an employer. I have yet to encounter a management team with extra time on their hands, or a team dying to get in between an employee and their doctor. I am not suggesting that to have a TCHP an employer needs to spend significantly more time managing their plan themselves and I am definitely not suggesting that an employer needs to start making health care decisions on behalf of their employees.

What must happen, however, is that an employer needs to change their mindset and keep the following concepts front and center:

- It is absolutely possible to manage the health care supply chain.

- The health care system is incredibly complex and although end users want to do the right thing, they often don't have the information to do so.
- There are creative and innovative partners available to do the heavy lifting.
- Uncontrolled cost increases are unacceptable and there is a better way.

Management from an employer perspective surrounding a TCHP falls into two categories:
1. Playing the role of conductor, making sure that the right partners are in the right seats and that the right results are being realized. It is very important, however, to ensure that the players are integrating well which is why an independent third party administrator is often the best solution for employers. They have based their business model on flexibility and partnering with many different vendors. While a carrier, on the other hand, may allow an employer to swap out certain pieces, the integration is often less than favorable.
2. Leading the messaging surrounding what is to be expected from a health insurance plan. I will mention this multiple times throughout this book, the message to plan participants is very simple: If you keep doing what you've always done, you'll keep getting what you've always got. With employees going backwards from an income standpoint, if delivered correctly there should be a favorable response to taking "total control" over the plan in search of different outcomes.

Examples of how an employer can play the conductor will be provided throughout this book, so for the remainder of this chapter I am going to focus on point 2. Of the concepts covered, this is the deepest of all of them. What should we expect from our health insurance plan? When pondering this question, it doesn't take long to picture yourself or someone you love stricken with a life-threatening condition and the desire to leave no stone unturned in search of the best possible outcome. You quickly find yourself in the midst of a philosophical debate that has been going on for as long as there has been health insurance. Should everything under the sun be covered with no caps on cost? Should there be a ROI calculator where the cost benefit analysis of a particular treatment is done? Ultimately, in the US, the conclusion we've come to is that it is ok to exclude coverage for certain items for various reasons, but in no way should a dollar amount be assigned to a particular life. The good news is for those desiring to implement a TCHP, you don't have to answer the deep philosophical questions. What you must do, however, is recalibrate your idea of health insurance as you know it today, and help your employees to do the same.

Health insurance as we know it today has its origins in the Health Maintenance Organization Act of 1973, which paved the way for the introduction of HMOs and other managed care plans. For those around long enough to remember, when HMOs were first introduced, they were considered a four letter word by many participants and in some areas of the country they still are today. Why was this, what was it that people had against the HMO and managed care? While the list may be endless, for the purposes of our discussion I'd like to focus on two things:
1. Participants were required to have a primary care physician who served as a gatekeeper to the health care system and coordinated their care.
2. There were limitations as to which providers participants could see.

Both of these strategies were logical in their origins. It made sense for physicians to serve in the role of a gatekeeper as they clearly had the training to understand what made sense when. Untrained individuals directing themselves through a complex and everchanging health care system were sure to lead to waste, inefficiency, and less than ideal results. Additionally, with costs beginning to rise, it made sense to seek out opportunities to reduce costs. As a result, the concept of a network was born where payers sought out discounted prices in return for steering business to select providers.

The issue is that, generally speaking, we don't like to be told what to do. As a result, as managed care plans evolved, two key things occurred. First, the requirement of a PCP serving in the role of a gatekeeper was eroded with more liberal plan designs like the PPO gaining market share and even HMOs started to eliminate the referral requirement as long as patients stayed in network. Second, as insurers competed with one another, one of the key differentiators between them became the size of their networks with the end result being the expansion of networks over time to the place we are today where it seems that most networks have just about every provider in them.

So why would managed care organizations allow these two things to happen? It is important to remember that all players, with the exception of rate payers and end users, are businesses. From a demand standpoint, the market forces pushing for a more user-friendly product were greater than the market forces demanding lower rates. If everyone is expanding their networks and increasing rates accordingly, there is little motivation to continue to offer a smaller network with greater controls.

At the same time that managed care was evolving to what we know today, another massive shift was occurring: the explosion of health care as a business. Compared to even 20 years ago, the treatments, technologies, and cures that have been developed are nothing short of incredible. Conditions that were once considered life-threatening or even terminal are now considered manageable and/or even curable. This is a wonderful thing, but there has been one massive flaw with the system. Unlike other areas of our economy that operate in a traditional market, the health care business operates in an alternate universe where the benefactors of the products largely don't foot the bill. Rather, the cost of the services are spread out over very large populations in the form of insurance. What this has allowed for is that every player in the health care supply chain is able to gradually or even dramatically inflate their prices as the impact is softened by spreading the cost out across the insured population.

According to the Kaiser Family Foundation, in 2017, 56% of the US population was covered by private insurance (49% employer sponsored, 7% individual coverage). That equates to roughly 185 million people to spread annual premium increases over.[8] As the increases have been gradual, generally speaking, the focus hasn't been to address the actual price of the services rendered. Rather, as premiums go up, the rate payers either absorb the increase or shift the cost off to someone else (i.e., employees) in the form of higher deductibles, co-pays, or premium contributions. At the same time, every other player in the health care supply chain has been steadily increasing costs and building thriving businesses.

Certainly you could argue that this is exactly what insurance is for, spreading out large unforeseen expenses over large populations. In concept that is true, but the health insurance market is unlike any other insurance market. Take homeowner's insurance, for example. The difference between homeowner's insurance and health insurance is that homes are built every day with consumers paying the cost directly, allowing market forces to work their magic. If the vast majority of homes were built with insurance policies paying for them, it is most likely costs would be significantly higher as would be the associated insurance premiums. With health insurance, on the other hand, a relatively small percentage of the

---

[8] Henry J. Kaiser Family Foundation, "Health Insurance Coverage of the Total Population," accessed April 15, 2018: https://www.kff.org/other/state-indicator/total-population/?currentTimeframe=0&sortModel=%7B%22colId%22:%22Location%22,%22sort%22:%22asc%22%7D.

expenses are paid directly by the end user. This removes the impact of market forces and allows costs to increase unimpeded.

Another point of comparison is what has happened with lasik eye surgery since it was introduced. Traditionally seen as a cosmetic procedure and therefore considered elective and excluded from insurance coverage, this procedure has evolved to a very refined procedure while at the same time coming down in cost. As far as health care is concerned, it is a rare exception.

For years this model has moved along without much resistance as the impacts were relatively incremental year over year, at least until now. We have finally reached the point where the two players in the health care supply chain who aren't in business, the rate payers and the end users, are starting to say "enough." The common strategy of shifting cost by increasing premium or decreasing benefits has gotten to the end of its run. As PWC points out in their trend forecast for 2018, "any meaningful impact on cost over time is going to have focus as much on price as utilization."[9] At some point, someone has to say "no."

What does that look like? Am I suggesting that employers and their self-insured plans become the HMOs of the 1970s and 1980s? Not at all, but I am suggesting that plans need to be managed like any other supply chain. Today, as my NextGen Benefits Mastermind Partnership colleague, Andy Neary pointed out, "the health insurance card in your employee's wallet is basically like an unlimited credit card."[10] Sure, depending on your plan design, there may be cost containment features built into it, but for the most part, it is an unlimited credit card.

---

[9] https://www.pwc.com/us/en/health-industries/health-research-institute/behind-the-numbers/reports/hri-behind-the-numbers-2018.pdf, page 7, accessed June 2018.
[10] Andy Neary, NextGen Benefits Mastermind Partnership, personal quote.

A close friend of mine has built a highly successful IT consulting firm, and I recently asked him about the process his clients go through when upgrading their IT infrastructure. I posed the following question to him, "when your clients need to buy computers do they just pick someone off of the line, give them a credit card, and send them off to wherever they want to buy new computers?" As you might suspect, his answer was "absolutely not, that would be crazy!" He explained to me that the process was very methodical and well thought out. First the IT contact within the company works internally to identify what the exact needs of the organization are and what the budget is. They then work with the IT firm to identify the best solutions to meet those needs. Finally, the IT firm solicits numerous bids and negotiates the best pricing to complete the project.

This shouldn't come as a surprise to anyone reading this book, but it does make one wonder why, with health insurance, are employers perfectly comfortable giving employees a blank credit card when they wouldn't do it in any other setting. The remainder of this chapter will outline how effective management of your plan can still provide all the benefits to your employees that they have grown accustomed to, while at the same time driving down the price of services you are buying.

As I stated earlier, effectively managing your plan requires a change of mindset. Generally speaking, both employees and their employers have come to expect health insurance to cover whatever whenever, and it is this inattention that has allowed costs to skyrocket. When looking at all other aspects of a business, this laissez-faire attitude is unique to health insurance.

Take for example, employee travel. The majority of businesses I've encountered establish budgets for employees for travel expenses like hotels, rental cars, meals, and client entertainment. If an employee always stayed at the Ritz, rented exotic cars, ate at the finest restaurants, and spent unlimited sums of money entertaining clients, someone at some point would notice and likely put a stop to it. While employee travel and treatments for life-threatening conditions are vastly different things, the underlying management principles should be very much the same.

Ok, so you've bought into the concept that a health insurance plan needs to be managed like other aspects of the business. Isn't this what you pay your administrator for, and if not, how does an employer effectively manage the plan without getting in between employees and their doctors? I'll address the first question first. If your health insurance gets more expensive each year and the only solutions you've been presented to address the cost is to shift more cost to the end user, then your current administrator is not effectively managing your plan.

To address the second question, there are dozens of unique, strategically-minded companies that exist solely to help employers manage certain aspects of their plan. Armed with the data referenced in Chapter 3, you will be able to identify exactly where your plan needs more effective management. Then, with the help of a next generation benefit advisor, you will be able to partner with the ideal vendor to address your particular challenges. Let me give you an example.

If you lift up the hood of the majority of health insurance plans, you will see something labeled "medical management." Unfortunately, unlike the oil filler cap on an internal combustion engine, what you'll find under the medical management cap varies dramatically from plan to plan.

On the surface, medical management is the process of a case manager (commonly a registered nurse) working with a patient before (ideally) or after a claim to ensure the best outcomes and ideally a lower cost. While the strategy is largely the same from plan to plan, the execution of the strategy is where the gains are made. Take, for example, simply the number of resources deployed. On average across the industry, here are the numbers:

- Carriers: Roughly 1 nurse per 50,0000 to 60,000 patients and 1 percent of the population is reached.
- TPAs: Roughly 1 nurse per 20,000 patients and 5 percent of the population is reached.
- Independent Specialty Medical Management Firms: Roughly 1 nurse per 5,000 patients and 20 percent of the population is reached.

Using the old 80/20 rule, which states that 80 percent of your claims come from 20 percent of your population, which model do you believe would be most effective in achieving the desired results? Do you know what the ratio of nurses to patients is with your current plan?

It isn't simply the number of people on the front line that makes the difference, but it is also what they are doing when they get there. Deb Ault, the founder of Ault International Medical Management (AIMM) and a Registered Nurse, is the perfect case study for this. A former drill sergeant, Nurse Deb as she likes to be called, started AIMM after working for the competition for years. Frustrated by the lack of results, she knew there was a better way.

AIMM defines medical management as "helping patients to move through the health plan and health care delivery system," and they serve as the nerve center of an effectively managed plan because they touch nearly every claim. From an employee perspective, AIMM serves as a concierge, helping employees navigate the health care system to achieve the best possible outcome. After all, isn't this what the patient wants? As health insurance plans stand today, patients have become conditioned to believe that the only way to ensure the best possible outcome is to have access to all providers and all services at all times. In reality, however, the exact opposite is true.

This is where you, the employer, must work to start changing the mindset of your employees. Employees must know that everything you are doing to effectively manage your plan is driven by two inextricably linked goals: to deliver the best possible outcome as cost effectively as possible. Your plan is no longer going to be solely focused on delivering the best possible outcome regardless of costs, nor is it going to focus on delivering every service at the lowest cost.

The second way that AIMM serves their customers is by filling a massive void that currently exists. In his 2007 Wall Street Journal article titled, "How Many Doctors Does It Take to Treat a Patient?" Peter Bach outlines the issue like this:

This spring my colleagues and I published a study of Medicare in the New England Journal of Medicine, *showing that what happened in the Chicago suburbs actually happens nationwide. Medicare patients bounce between many doctors, most of whom are unaffiliated with one another and, as a result, few patients have a single doctor who is central to the care they receive.*

The typical Medicare patient in one year sees seven different doctors, including five different specialists, working in four different practices. For vulnerable patients with multiple chronic conditions, care is even more fragmented and involves more doctors. Forty percent of the patients in our study had seven or more chronic conditions and they saw on average 11 doctors in seven practices; the upper quartile of this group saw 16 or more different doctors in nine or more different practices.

Health care is like this because of the way doctors are paid. Few doctors receive an hourly rate or a set annual salary; most are paid according to a system called "fee for service," in which visits, tests and procedures are reimbursed separately. Doctors face incentives to provide more services and more expensive services, and so they do just that.

The government's finding that spending is rising could be seen as evidence that more patients are benefiting from the best medicine has to offer. But another government report, from the Agency for Healthcare Research and Quality, has a different message. Despite seeing many doctors, few patients get the treatments that are recommended for them, and few have their chronic diseases well-managed. For example, fewer than 30% of people with high blood pressure have it adequately controlled, according to the agency's most recent analysis of health-care quality. No surprise, really. Fee for service incentives are linked to the number of services doctors provide, not the quality of those services.

Perhaps then our study's findings could be interpreted as a boon for patient choice? Not likely. From a clinical perspective, 16 or 11 or even seven different doctors treating a patient is no way to deliver high quality care. Patients are best served when they have at most a few physicians who work together to develop and monitor a cohesive coordinated plan of care.[11]

Today, most plans lack someone who is thinking about the big picture every time a service is ordered. Additionally, it is unacceptable for someone to be able to name their mechanic, but not their primary care physician. Everyone needs to have one because if they don't, they are highly likely to seek far more expensive avenues for care when the need arises. A plan with effective medical management will ensure that each member has a PCP by serving as their concierge and walking them through the process of establishing a relationship with one.

---

[11] Peter B. Bach, "How Many Doctors Does It Take to Treat a Patient?" The Wall Street Journal, June 21, 2017, A17.

From a messaging standpoint, an employer needs to drive this point home. Total Control Health Plans are about being smart about how the plan is built, designed, and used. They are a departure from the cruise control unlimited credit card of the past, and to work there must be honest conversations from adults to adults about how a TCHP is changing the status quo.

Finally, to add icing on the cake, books have been written about whether physicians should know about or even care about price whenever they order a service or make a referral. I can absolutely appreciate the arguments in favor of physicians being blind to cost, however, if no one is paying attention, then we end up with a reality like we have today. In addition to the philosophical arguments in favor of physicians being blind to cost, the reality is that they also have many other factors influencing the decisions that they make. Whether it be a physician who is employed by a health care system being contractually or financially required to refer within the same system or concerns about malpractice claims, an effectively managed plan must have another set of eyes coordinating the care to ensure the best possible outcomes as cost effectively as possible.

So, does medical management actually achieve the desired results? Milliman Care Guidelines, LLC, a subsidiary of Milliman, believe that it does. By extrapolating their 2016 Milliman Care Guidelines, which are independently developed and produced evidence-based clinical guidelines and software used to support the care management of a majority of Americans depending on the level of management, a plan should cost the following:

Medical and Rx approved claims, per employee per year:
- Severely Broken - $17,000
- Moderately Broken - $14,000
- Relatively Broken - $11,034
- Loosely Managed - $10,800
- Moderately Managed - $8,300

- Well Managed - $6,500[12]

Ok, but those are actuarial estimates, what happens in real life? Across the AIMM book of business for all well-managed clients, the total medical and Rx approved claims per employee per year was $6,500 and it is projected to go down by 3.8% in 2018.

Fine, management works but I can save money by just saying "no" too. Here's the thing, AIMM isn't saying no, but rather they are using common sense strategies to effectively manage a plan. For example, most of the employers reading this book likely have an Employee Assistance Program, which provides mental health and other services to employees and their dependents. Employers have either elected to purchase an EAP directly, or get it as an add-on from one of the insurance companies they work with. While the benefits in EAPs vary, most of them include 3–5 outpatient mental health counseling sessions per beneficiary per year. Knowing this, AIMM works with employers to ensure that the health insurance plan includes language requiring the exhaustion of the EAP mental health benefits before the health insurance plan will cover any outpatient mental health benefits. When a claim of this nature comes in for prior authorization, AIMM reaches out to the patient directly to explain the benefit and assist them in scheduling their first visit through the EAP. This is just common sense: leveraging an existing benefit, which historically has a miserable utilization rate of 5% or less, to contain costs for the health insurance plan.

You might say "my plan has disease management built into it, isn't that the same thing?" No, it isn't. Similar to medical management, disease management can have multiple definitions, but for the purpose of our discussion we will define disease management as efforts to assist members in the management of a chronic condition. For example, disease management related to diabetes would include outreach to the member to ensure he or she has met

---

[12] Milliman Care Guidelines, "Industry-Leading Evidence-Based Care Guidelines," extrapolated by Deb Ault.

all of the standards of care for that condition, such as having their A1c regularly checked. While not a new concept, disease management as a cost containment strategy has gotten significantly more attention over the last 7–8 years as the data available has gotten better. I'm going to say something pretty controversial next, so if you aren't sitting down, please go ahead and do so.

Disease management may not necessarily be a good cost containment strategy for your plan. There, I said it. Let me explain. The logic behind disease management is that by leveraging data and outreach, a plan will proactively pay smaller claims in the hope of preventing or at least delaying much larger claims. This makes sense…unless the population on your plan only stays there for a year or two. If the turnover on your plan is significantly high, and you are focused on aggressive disease management, what you are doing in reality is investing in healthier employees for their next employer. This would be the equivalent of utilizing more expensive fully synthetic oil to ensure better performance at high mileage, in a fleet of cars that you lease and turn over every two years.

I am not equating individual human beings to cars and trucks, but the point that I am making is that someone in a business would absolutely consider the ROI on using more expensive synthetic oil in their fleet before doing so. The same should be done with a health insurance plan. If, after considering the ROI from implementing an aggressive disease management program, an employer elects to do so, great, it is a good thing. Some employers may even determine this is an investment they don't expect a ROI simply because it is the right thing to do. Awesome, that's great too. The bottom line is that an employer should put themselves in a position to review the relevant information to make an informed decision about items like this. That is how you achieve a Total Control Health Plan.

As you dive in and set your business on the course to a TCHP, you will quickly find that there are far more levers to pull to effectively manage your plan than you previously thought. You will identify that there are some that you have no interest in pulling due to lack of ROI, or simply for philosophical reasons. What is important is that the leadership within your business understands why the decisions are made and the impact from doing so, which is a significant departure from the reality most employers have faced for too long.

Chapter 5
Access to Information

It likely goes without saying, but the key to effectively managing anything is having access to meaningful information. As leaders of your business, you are in a constant quest for more information to better inform the decisions you make. Many of you likely believe that you have done the same thing in relation to managing your health insurance plan. You've sought out as much information as possible from your vendors and trusted advisors, and then made the best decision you could. Short of having a self-insured health care plan with an independent TPA however, the type of information you've been given, I would argue, hasn't been very meaningful. It has been more transactional in nature, such as this carrier is cheaper than that carrier for the same plan, or if you do this to your plan design it will reduce the increase by 2%. Rarely does the information made available to you answer the "why" behind any of the meaningful questions you'd like to ask.

Have you ever had a conversation like this with your advisor or health insurance carrier?
"Trend is 8% this year."
"Why?"
"Because health care costs are going up."
"Why?"
"Because things are getting more expensive."
"Why?"
"Because companies are charging more for the same things this year."

Or how about one like this?
"Trend is 8% this year, but you are getting a 2% increase."
"That's great, but why?"
"Because your plan ran well."
"Awesome, but why? Were we just lucky?"
"Your claims were lower than what we thought you'd have. Pretty cool huh?"
"But why?"
"Pretty cool, isn't it?"

Or how about this one?
"Trend is 8% and your plan ran really poorly last year, but you are getting a 5% increase."
"That's strange, why is that?"
"It could have been 14%, but it isn't."
"Why?"
"5%, pretty cool, huh?"

Over the last 17 years that I've been advising employers, I've been part of many conversations like that. I'm the type of person who needs to understand the why behind something, I can't just take something at face value. For the first few years, I'd try to get to the why so that I could accurately explain it to my customers, and often I'd find myself wanting to bang my head against the wall as I simply couldn't get a clear and concise explanation for the why behind many perplexing renewal-related scenarios that I came across. Eventually I just gave up and invited the carrier(s) in to tell the story. My clients and I would sit on one side of the table, with the representative from the insurance company on the other side and we'd have conversations like the examples above. At the end of the meeting, we'd often feel dumber than at the outset of the discussion. This isn't to blame the carrier representatives, they were simply repeating the same corporate explanations that they were trained to give.

Here's the deal—insurance is a business and it isn't rocket surgery. Insurance carriers make decisions all the time that seem illogical, but are made for business reasons. For example, an insurance company might elect to pass along a small increase or even a rate decrease to a prominent employer in the market, even if the plan performance doesn't call for it. This would be done for business reasons, which is perfectly justifiable. The issue with this, in my opinion, is that you can't bank on the generosity of an insurance company as your primary strategy for addressing the cost of your plan. As many others have said before, hope is not a strategy. The flow of information from carriers/administrators to the employer plan sponsors is more often than not incomplete at best resulting in a "take our word for it" reality. There is no way for an employer to effectively manage anything, if they don't understand the basic cause and effect. If you get a 2% increase one year, and absolutely nothing changes the next year and you get a 15% increase, how on earth can you do anything to control what happens the following year? I have worked with many employers, both large and small, who approach renewals like the old game show, Press Your Luck. They would sit across the table from me muttering "No Whammies, No Whammies, No Whammies," because their insurance carrier, and therefore I, had no meaningful information to give them. This isn't a way to live!

There are many reasons carriers don't release all of the information possible, some of which will be covered in this chapter, but the fact is that any employer who aspires to have a Total Control Health Plan must have access to lots of meaningful information, and equally important, they need to know what to do with it once they get it. The goods news is, I've seen it! It really does exist and employers all over the country are getting their hands on it, today.

The Basics

As referenced before, the cost of health insurance is expensive because the cost of health care is expensive, so let's dive into that more deeply. According to the Milliman Medical Index, "in 2017, the cost of healthcare for a typical American family of four covered by an average employer-sponsored preferred provider organization (PPO) plan is $26,944."[13] Additionally, "there are two major components to the cost of care: the amount paid for each type of service and the frequency with which each type of service is used."[14]

Therefore, an employer who desires to impact the cost of their health insurance plan must understand the drivers behind what is getting consumed and why. According to Milliman, medical services fall into five primary categories:
1. Inpatient Care - 31%
2. Outpatient Care - 19%
3. Professional services (Physicians) - 30%
4. Pharmacy - 17%
5. Other (i.e., ambulance, etc.) - 4%

Put simply, a Total Control Health Plan is one where an employer knows what is driving the utilization, the price of the various services in each category, and has a strategy to effectively manage each category. This isn't to say that each employer is managing each category themselves, but rather they have solid relationships with trusted partners who effectively and transparently manage each category of care.

---

[13] Christopher S. Girod, Susan K. Hart, Scott A. Weltz, "2017 Milliman Medical Index," (Milliman May 16, 2017), accessed April 25, 2018: http://www.milliman.com/insight/Periodicals/mmi/2017-Milliman-Medical-Index/.
[14] Ibid.

This is a good spot to revisit a phrase I used in the introduction: health care supply chain. When you think about all of the links in the health care supply chain, there are only two links where their participation isn't their primary business. From hospitals to pharmaceutical manufacturers and doctors to health insurers, they are all largely paid by insurance companies and indirectly the end user (patient) or the rate payers. I am not pointing this out because it is a bad thing, but rather to make the point that the vast majority of the players in the health care supply chain are run by smart, effective business leaders who have shareholders and boards to which they report. As an example of what I mean by this, review Table 5.1. This table outlines the stock price of the five major for-profit health insurance carriers compared to the Dow Jones and S&P prior to the passage of the Affordable Care Act and as of January, 2018. From an investor's point of view, this is fantastic, but from the perspective of the rate payer is it possible something is a bit off?

	UHC	Cigna	Humana	Aetna	Anthem	Dow Jones	S&P 500
3/4/2010	$33.16	$36.94	$49.02	$34.99	$63.61	10,888.83	1,174.17
1/26/2018	$248.47	$226.22	$288.29	$193.10	$258.19	$26,616.17	$2,839.25
% Change	649%	512%	488%	452%	306%	144%	142%

Table 5.1

Understanding, with the exception of the rate payer and end user, that every player in the supply chain in a business is key to understanding the value of a Total Control Health Plan. Therefore, the foundation of a TCHP is information. Depending on the size of your health insurance plan today, you either have no information at all about your plan other than who is enrolled in it, or you may have some information about how your plan is running, but you likely don't know how to use that information in a meaningful way.

HIPAA

One of the most commonly used tactics related to releasing information to a plan sponsor by a plan administrator is referencing the Health Insurance Portability and Accountability Act (HIPAA) and its restriction on releasing Protected Health Information (PHI). For example, one of the key components used in developing the premium rates for an experience rated fully insured group, or a self-insured plan, are the details surrounding plan participants who are expected to incur claims over a certain threshold, such as $20,000. Accessing information, such as diagnosis, prognosis, and case management notes, are key components to projecting future costs and also identifying strategies to provide the best possible care at the lowest possible cost. This information is the equivalent of reviewing someone's driving record prior to issuing auto insurance, or their credit rating prior to approving a loan.

In the case of the typical health insurance plan, however, especially those administered by a commercial carrier as opposed to those administered by an independent third party administrator, this information is exceedingly difficult to obtain. I can appreciate the concern this particular topic may have with those responsible for overseeing an employer-sponsored health insurance plan. With few exceptions, of the business leaders I have worked with over the years, none of them want to dive into the personal health of their colleagues and families nor do they want to be in a position to determine who can get what from a treatment standpoint. Let me be clear, I am not suggesting an employer should be involved in determining who gets what, however, I am stating unequivocally that those managing a plan can have access to this information and it is absolutely required to effectively manage the plan. Without information of this sort, employers have no way of validating the claims made by their insurers and/or administrators, nor can they be sure that the best possible care is being delivered at the lowest possible cost. Stated another way, they have no control.

Later, this chapter will dive more deeply into how an employer can achieve total control over their health insurance plan while avoiding the concerns addressed earlier. Before that, however, I must dispel once and for all the HIPAA PHI myth. Running the risk of getting too technical, the following is taken directly from the Health and Human Services website, specifically outlining appropriate uses of protected health information:

A Covered Entity is one of the following:
- A Health Care Provider (this includes providers such as doctors, clinics, psychologists, dentists, chiropractors, nursing homes, pharmacies…but only if they transmit any information in an electronic form in connection with a transaction for which HHS has adopted a standard)
- A Health Plan (this includes health insurance companies, HMOs, company health plans, government programs that pay for health care, such as Medicare, Medicaid, and the military and veterans health care programs)
- A Health Care Clearinghouse (this includes entities that process nonstandard health information they receive from another entity into a standard [i.e., standard electronic format or data content] or vice versa)[15]

Uses and Disclosures for Treatment, Payment, and Health Care Operations
45 CFR 164.506

---

[15] https://www.hhs.gov/hipaa/for-professionals/covered-entities/index.html, accessed June 2018.

Background

The HIPAA Privacy Rule establishes a foundation of Federal protection for personal health information, carefully balanced to avoid creating unnecessary barriers to the delivery of quality health care. As such, the Rule generally prohibits a covered entity from using or disclosing protected health information unless authorized by patients, except where this prohibition would result in unnecessary interference with access to quality health care or with certain other important public benefits or national priorities. Ready access to treatment and efficient payment for health care, both of which require use and disclosure of protected health information, are essential to the effective operation of the health care system. In addition, certain health care operations—such as administrative, financial, legal, and quality improvement activities—conducted by or for health care providers and health plans, are essential to support treatment and payment. Many individuals expect that their health information will be used and disclosed as necessary to treat them, bill for treatment, and, to some extent, operate the covered entity's health care business. To avoid interfering with an individual's access to quality health care or the efficient payment for such health care, the Privacy Rule permits a covered entity to use and disclose protected health information, with certain limits and protections, for treatment, payment, and health care operations activities.

How the Rule Works

What are Treatment, Payment, and Health Care Operations? The core health care activities of "Treatment," "Payment," and "Health Care Operations" are defined in the Privacy Rule at 45 CFR 164.501.

- *"Treatment" generally means the provision, coordination, or management of health care and related services among health care providers or by a health care provider with a third party, consultation between health care providers regarding a patient, or the referral of a patient from one health care provider to another.*
- *"Payment" encompasses the various activities of health care providers to obtain payment or be reimbursed for their services and of a health plan to obtain premiums, to fulfill their coverage responsibilities and provide benefits under the plan, and to obtain or provide reimbursement for the provision of health care. In addition to the general definition, the Privacy Rule provides examples of common payment activities which include, but are not limited to:*

  Determining eligibility or coverage under a plan and adjudicating claims;

  Risk adjustments;

  Billing and collection activities;

  Reviewing health care services for medical necessity, coverage, justification of charges, and the like;

  Utilization review activities; and

  Disclosures to consumer reporting agencies (limited to specified identifying information about the individual, his or her payment history, and identifying information about the covered entity).
- *"Health care operations" are certain administrative, financial, legal, and quality improvement activities of a covered entity that are necessary to run its business and to support the core functions of treatment and payment. These activities, which are limited to the activities listed in the definition of "health care operations" at 45 CFR 164.501, include:*

  Conducting quality assessment and improvement activities, population-based activities relating to improving health or reducing health care costs, and case management and care coordination;

Reviewing the competence or qualifications of health care professionals, evaluating provider and health plan performance, training health care and non-health care professionals, accreditation, certification, licensing, or credentialing activities;

Underwriting and other activities relating to the creation, renewal, or replacement of a contract of health insurance or health benefits, and ceding, securing, or placing a contract for reinsurance of risk relating to health care claims

Conducting or arranging for medical review, legal, and auditing services, including fraud and abuse detection and compliance programs;

Business planning and development, such as conducting cost-management and planning analyses related to managing and operating the entity; and

Business management and general administrative activities, including those related to implementing and complying with the Privacy Rule and other Administrative Simplification Rules, customer service, resolution of internal grievances, sale or transfer of assets, creating de-identified health information or a limited data set, and fundraising for the benefit of the covered entity. General Provisions at 45 CFR 164.506.

A covered entity may, without the individual's authorization:

- *Use or disclose protected health information for its own treatment, payment, and health care operations activities. For example:*

    A hospital may use protected health information about an individual to provide health care to the

> *individual and may consult with other health care providers about the individual's treatment.*
>
> *A health care provider may disclose protected health information about an individual as part of a claim for payment to a health plan.*
>
> *A health plan may use protected health information to provide customer service to its enrollees.*

Over the last 17 years that I've been working with employer-sponsored health insurance plans, I have seen two distinctly different answers given when the specific details on claimants are requested.

1. The first, and more common answer that I've been given is that they are only able to release general, de-identified information due to HIPAA constraints. As covered above, this is 100% inaccurate, but it doesn't stop the administrator from repeating the answer.
2. The second response that I have seen is detailed information on diagnosis, prognosis, and even case management notes outlining the specific details of the patient's condition. For example, "Nurse X spoke with patient on 10/24/17, and discussed the progress of the treatment plan and things are going very well. Nurse X also spoke with treating physician on 10/25/17, and they stated treatment is progressing better than expected."

Which answer do you believe would be more meaningful for an employer looking to make decisions about how best to manage their plan? With the exception of employers with fully-insured plans that are community rated (i.e., all employers are lumped together in a large pool), if you have gotten something resembling answer 1, you do not have a Total Control Health Plan.

Let me reinforce the point.

Case Study

Within the last two years I was working with a client with approximately 400 employees on their health insurance plan. The company was contemplating transitioning from a fully-insured plan to a self-insured plan. Approximately six months prior to their potential go-live date of the new plan, it was revealed to them through a meeting with their current carrier that there was a member on the plan with an extremely expensive medication, one that was projected to cost over $750,000 in one year. To the carrier's credit, they did share the name of the drug, however very little else would be released, such as prognosis, who the claimant was, etc. "due to HIPAA restrictions."

Now why would an employer need to know who it was? I am in no way suggesting that this employer, or any employer, would make decisions surrounding how to manage their plan that would target any particular individual. This is illegal. What if, however, by knowing who the claimant was, additional information may be brought to light that could inform decision making. For example, what if it were known that the particular individual in question was scheduled to retire in a few months, or was relocating and taking a new job? Knowing this sort of information may lead an employer to make drastically different decisions about how best to manage their plan if it was available to them. The exact same thing could be said about having prognosis information.

In this particular case, armed with the name of the drug, I was able to conduct extensive research into what it treats, projected future costs, and develop strategies to ensure the patient continued to receive the medication while mitigating the exposure to the plan. In the end, I was able to identify a strategy that mitigated the risk (i.e., cost) to the plan for all claims of this nature while not putting any individual with a similar claim at any additional financial risk. That was an ideal outcome.

The need for information isn't simply limited to having details about the particular claims within your plan, which impact what your plan buys and why, but those hoping to have a meaningful impact on the performance of their plan also need a lot of information about price. In addition to needing price information to effectively control costs, those responsible for managing a self-insured plan also have a fiduciary obligation to do so in a responsible way. It has been successfully argued in a growing number of lawsuits that employers have not met their fiduciary duties to the plan as they simply have no idea how the plan assets are spent.

Data Analytics

I had to do it. I couldn't write a book about business health insurance and not throw in some trendy catch phrases. Big data, predictive modeling, data warehouse, artificial intelligence—if you spend any time researching insurance advisors and insurance companies, you will run into one or all of these phrases very quickly. Just for fun, Google "health insurance predictive modeling."

Take this unaltered paragraph from a recent article:

Meanwhile, Jonathan Slotkin, M.D., director of spinal surgery in the Geisinger Health System Neurosciences Institute, also serves as medical director of Geisinger in Motion, a department focusing on digital engagement and patient- and provider-facing mobile device technologies, within the division of informatics at the health system. Slotkin helps lead the informatics work that underlies the Fresh Food Farmacy project. "For me," he told Landi, "it's fascinating from an informatics standpoint because it brings together traditional clinical care, which we've all gotten pretty good at, but it also brings in the harder issues around data and the transactional level of social determinants of health, costing, supply chain and distribution, things that most medical systems are not yet optimized for. I think as we all endeavor to manage and help our populations with social determinants of health, we are going to be faced with these challenges more and more."[16]

Bam, lower costs dead ahead.

I am making fun of the terms as just about everyone in the health care and health insurance industry uses them in some way today, but other than being great on a brochure, what the heck does it mean for an employer? Just like Amazon being able to predict that I am going to like *Blue Ocean Strategy* because I've read books by Daniel Pink, health insurance carriers and administrators can use data and predictive modeling to identify where future claims are going to come from and take steps to mitigate those claims. The concept is fantastic, rather than looking in the rearview mirror, we are looking through the windshield anticipating what is coming next.

As I've already stated, almost all players in the health insurance market have some sort of data warehouse and predictive modeling capabilities. That being said, with few exceptions, I have seen very little tangible positive impact as a result. Don't get me wrong, I believe in the concept and I absolutely believe it can and will continue to help control costs, but if everyone is already doing it, then why aren't costs going down? My belief is that while carriers are using data to identify those patients who could benefit from early intervention, there simply aren't enough soldiers on the front line to have a meaningful impact on your particular plan. It isn't the data that is failing, it is the execution.

Here is an example. Five years ago, I was working with an employer with approximately 700 employees spread out among roughly 5–7 states. The company was looking for a new self-insured plan administrator. Ultimately, they selected one of the big

---

[16] https://www.healthcare-informatics.com/article/analytics/can-prescription-fresh-food-treat-diabetes-geisinger-analytics-driven-project, accessed June 2018.

national players, with one key reason being the predictive modeling technology they were promised. The pitch was that they bounce the claims data that accumulated over the first year against a massive database of millions of claims to, in effect, play the tape forward. By comparing existing claims today against similar claims from the past, the tool could predict where today's claimant would be in the future if nothing was done. They would then use this data to assign a risk score to each plan participant, and then focus intensive outreach and management efforts on those with the highest score and/or the greatest potential for ROI. After year one, we all sat on the edge of our seats as we eagerly anticipated the release of the first scoring report. To say that what was produced was underwhelming, is putting it mildly. Not only was the data itself basic and uninspiring, but the actions taken by the administrator to address those at greatest risk failed with little more than a whimper. It was our expectation that, as promised, we'd be receiving detailed reporting about what specific actions were taken to establish contact with each high-risk individual and what the fruits of those efforts were. In reality, the outreach largely consisted of "monitoring" and mailings. As time went by, we continued to push for more detailed reporting and meaningful proof of effective interventions, but nothing ever came. Unfortunately, I've seen this happen more than once, with many different carriers and administrators.

The good news is that the future is here. There are partners today who can make the dream a reality. Not only can they produce meaningful predictive modeling, but they can get it across the finish line by actually having meaningful engagements with those members who are at risk, or at least informing those who can. Employers must be sure that the partners they've selected to help them manage their plan are doing everything they can to achieve the desired results of the best care at the lowest possible cost. It can be done and is being done today, but far too often the execution doesn't go beyond the brochure.

In addition to having a management mindset toward their health plan, Total Control Health Plan sponsors must have an unending thirst for information. They must do their due diligence and ensure that if they aren't getting the information they need, they pursue alternative options. TCHPs administered by the right independent third party administrator have the ability to interchange different partners until the desired result is reached. With costs continuing to rise unabated, it is absolutely unacceptable to not be able to answer the "why" behind your plan's performance. The answers exist and employers are finding them every day. If you don't have them, you need to make a change.

Case Study: Peoria Public Schools

When Peoria Public Schools began working with AIMM, the medical cost PMPM was close to $500. The group was eager to avoid cost-shifting and benefit erosion, committed to providing the highest quality of care, and also wanted to control cost. Due to AIMM's ability to focus on the needs of high-risk members and manage behavior change, Peoria Public Schools benefited from improved member health and reduced costs. Within three years, the medical cost PMPM has decreased by 25%.

Health care costs are rising and creating more pressure on employers. Predictive modeling can help relieve that pressure with tools to 1) identify health risks in a given population, 2) quantify their impact on health benefit costs, and 3) measure the effectiveness of programs in lowering those costs. The analytics also prioritize individuals and determine the best approach to each person based on that individual's motivation to change.

When discussing the Peoria Public School results with Deb Ault she explained, "We've been easily able to move beyond the industry norm of reactive or real-time or even proactive medical management to delivering Predictive Care Management. Through predictive modeling we can engage members in advance of serious health issues to enhance their quality of care and quality of life. We all know healthier people file fewer claims. This tool, however, helps us solve the timing problem associated with investments in health and wellness initiatives. Most groups are not in a position to invest now on a return they will receive three or more years in the future. This tool lets us intervene now with patients who are one year return on investment situations."[17]

Author's note: The results outlined above are not simply the result of leveraging data, but doing so in a very aggressive way. As previously outlined, a best-in-class medical management firm has a ratio of 1 nurse per 5,000 plan participants and they reach at least 20% of the population. It is a must to have enough boots on the ground to leverage the data now available for your plan.

Expert Tip: Getting access data is only half the battle, knowing what to do with it when you get it is equally important. If you have a larger fully-insured plan or a self-insured plan and you've sat through a renewal meeting, then you've likely been presented with some reports. I've sat through hundreds of these meetings where a stack of reports are provided to the employer, with "data" that compares the employer's plan to the carrier book of business or some other benchmarking metric. Data points like male/female mix, average age, generic utilization rate, ER admits per 1,000, etc. are all referenced. If the number is more favorable than the benchmark everyone applauds, and if it is worse than the benchmark, a little head scratching and group nodding happens and then the discussion moves on. Think about that meeting with your administrator. Have you ever gotten a meaningful strategy to address the unfavorable numbers, or have you gotten any follow up that the administrator was actually doing something to address it

---

[17] Risk Managers, "School District Adopts Cost Saving Strategies – Reduces Costs 25%" (Blog, February 11, 2018), accessed April 25, 2018: http://blog.riskmanagers.us/?p=27085.

and it was working? Neither have I. The reason is that representatives from the administrator that you are meeting with are likely salespeople who know that they simply need to get through the meeting and few, if any, of their clients will revisit the discussion again.

While business leaders are extremely busy and pulled in many directions, those wanting to have a meaningful impact on the cost of their health insurance must stay focused on the task at hand. If you don't clearly understand the "why" behind your plan performance, then you must keep pushing until you do.

Chapter 6
Access to Providers

For the last 25 years, the vast majority of health insurance plans have been built around the concept of a network of providers. Whether a HMO, PPO, POS, or EPO, the network has been the foundational cost containment strategy used by health insurance plans. On the surface the concept of the network is very logical, the health insurance plan will steer patients to certain providers in return for discounts on the services rendered. Plans want to pay wholesale, not retail. While a good concept in theory, the lack of transparency surrounding networks and the contracts they implement with providers has lead to a backwards system where all players win as costs go up, with the exception of those who are footing the bill.

Anyone who has ever been involved in the process of shopping for a self-insured plan administrator knows that the number one item to review is the network discount being proposed. Commercial carriers and independent PPO networks compete on the size of their discount, promising plan sponsors greater savings through their network than the competition.

There are two major issues with this system, however. First, it is incredibly challenging for employers to validate the claims made by the carriers. This is due to the fact that while "discount" is a relatively straightforward term, carriers define it differently in an effort to inflate the value they provide to the plan sponsor. For example, some carriers include items such as duplicate or ineligible claims that weren't paid in their savings calculation. To me, I think getting credit for not doing something you shouldn't be doing is a bit too far. I explain this to my children all the time. Additionally, carriers/networks have differing levels of discount for facility and physician claims, and the definition of facility and physician claims vary from carrier to carrier. A facility claim for one is a physician claim for another, making a meaningful comparison very difficult to achieve. Compounding the issue is that the discounts vary from provider to provider making it next to impossible to project the actual savings a plan may realize through a particular network without also knowing exactly which claims are going to come from which providers.

To add to the fun, the contracts that carriers and standalone networks implement with the various providers to establish the discounts are highly confidential. Therefore, plan sponsors are left having to take their word for it, with no realistic way to validate the claims. While it is possible to conduct a "repricing analysis" with firms like Milliman where actual claims from a plan are run through the fee schedules of competing networks to get a meaningful comparison, in practice it is very time consuming and often cost prohibitive for plan sponsors to go through this exercise. The reality, that employers are then left with, is a plan that is buying services with absolutely no idea what the services cost. This is why plans are paying two identical claims to different providers and paying $150 at one and $1,500 at another. From a fiduciary standpoint, this is the equivalent of two retirement plan participants paying vastly different prices for the exact same stock on the same day at the same time. This wouldn't fly with a retirement plan, and it is starting to get noticed more and more with health insurance plans.

As I stated previously, there are two major issues with the network discount model that the majority of plans use, and the second is going to make the first seem minor in comparison. While there are multiple different models networks use to achieve a discount, the majority are based on a percentage discounted off of billed charges. When shopping for a plan administrator/network, this is the number that is thrown around all the time. "We have a 48% discount through our network!" Never mind that the 48% may include items like ineligible claims, the percentage sounds great. Employers and their advisors feel great about this, they are getting a massive discount on the claims and they quickly move on to talking about deductibles and co-pays. Here's the issue, whatever the discount is, it is based on *billed charges.*

Let's unpack that term a little. Billed charges are the "retail charges" a provider submits to an insurance plan for payment. It is the astronomically high number you see on your Explanation of Benefits right before the "approved amount" which is the amount actually paid by the plan. The billed charges originate from a hospital database called the Charge Description Master or Charge Master, which lists every possible item or service for which a patient could be billed. The prices listed on the Charge Master have no actual relation to cost, and are often many times higher. Additionally, the Charge Master is a living document that is updated regularly, in some cases as frequently as quarterly and at least annually. As you can imagine, rarely do the updates result in charges going down.

Evaluation & Management Services (CPT Codes 99201-99499)	2014 Average Charge	2015 Average Charge	2016 Average Charge
Emergency Room Visit, Level 2 (low to moderate severity)	$1,267	$1,445	$1,469
Emergency Room Visit, Level 3 (moderate severity)	$2,299	$2,621	$2,666
Emergency Room Visit, Level 4 (high severity)	$8,061	$9,190	$9,344
Laboratory & Pathology Services (CPT Codes 80047-89398)	Average Charge	Average Charge	Average Charge
Basic Metabolic Panel	$350	$350	$350
Blood Gas Analysis, including 02 saturation	$1,161	$1,324	$1,464
Complete Blood Count, automated	$285	$285	$285
Comprehensive Metabolic Panel	$435	$435	$435
Lipid Panel	$415	$415	$415
Partial Thromboplastin Time	$240	$274	$302
Prothrombin Time	$190	$217	$240
Troponin, Quantitative	$520	$593	$656
Urinalysis, with microscopy	$196	$196	$196
Radiology Services (CPT Codes 70010-79999)	Average Charge	Average Charge	Average Charge
CT Scan, Abdomen, with contrast	$6,285	$6,361	$6,857
CT Scan, Head or Brain, without contrast	$3,850	$4,136	$3,850
CT Scan, Pelvis, with contrast	$7,439	$8,831	$9,906
MRI, Head or Brain, without contrast, followed by contrast	$8,276	$8,486	$8,945
Ultrasound, Abdomen, Complete	$2,294	$2,161	$2,341
X-Ray, Chest, two views	$765	$716	$765
Medicine Services (CPT Codes 90281-99607)	Average Charge	Average Charge	Average Charge
Inhalation Treatment, pressurized or nonpressurized	$357	$407	$450
Physical Therapy, Evaluation	$692	$789	$867
Physical Therapy, Gait Training	$298	$340	$376
Physical Therapy, Therapeutic Exercise	$320	$365	$403
Surgery Services (CPT Codes 10021-69990)	Average Charge	Average Charge	Average Charge
Place Cath Carotd Art	$15,335	$20,893	$22,242
Ins Cath Abd/L-Ext Art 3rd	$7,294	$104,584	$54,308
Insert Tunneled Cv Cath	$5,382	$12,060	$12,240

Table 6.1

To illustrate this point, let's look at pricing information for Stanford University Hospital. The centers for Medicare and Medicaid services require all participating hospitals to report cost information annually and this information is then available to the public. One component includes the annual pricing information for the top 25 most common outpatient procedures at the facility. Table 6.1 outlines the pricing information for the top 25 at Stanford University Hospital in 2014, 2015, and 2016. As you will see, with very few exceptions the costs went up each year and in some cases went up dramatically. When accounting for fluctuations in volume, or any other factor other than rate increase, the annual increase in charges across the hospital was

$598,156,970 in 2014; $693,957,003 in 2015; and $785,073,594 in 2016.

Let's now think back to your employer-sponsored plan that is getting that incredible discount off of billed charges. From my perspective, it doesn't matter what percentage discount you are getting when the starting point is ratcheting up year over year over year. To add insult to injury, hospitals and carriers/networks actually have an incentive for the price to go up. With carriers/networks competing with each other to offer the biggest discounts to their clients, they approach providers pushing to get the best discount. Imagine this exchange taking place inside an insurance carrier's boardroom:

Carrier: "Listen, we are going to need a bigger discount from you to offer to our customers."

Hospital: "I'm sorry, but costs continue to go up for us and we simply can't afford to provide these services at a lower price. So, we can't give you a bigger discount."

Carrier: "I'm not sure you heard me correctly, so let me clarify. I need to be able to tell my customers that I have the biggest discount. I didn't say that I needed to tell them that I had the lowest price."

Hospital: "You know what, let me take a quick look at our Charge Master to see if I can find some room to give you a bigger discount. Well what do you know, after making a few adjustments to all of the prices, I am now able to offer you a 52% discount vs. the 48% we have today."

Carrier: "Great, we have a deal!"

While somewhat exaggerated, the story does a good job of illustrating the flaws with the existing model. While the idea of a discount is appealing, the reality is that without full transparency the "discount" isn't worth the paper it is printed on. Additionally, there are games that carriers can and do play all over the country that only make the situation worse. For example, the legislature in the State of Michigan had to take action and ban Most Favored Nation Clauses in 2013, because a carrier active in that state had negotiated these clauses into all of their hospital contracts with the end result being higher costs in return for a guarantee that no other carrier would receive a bigger discount.

Finally, to put a cherry on top, the Affordable Care Act has a built-in feature that incentivizes fully-insured carriers to favor higher claims. The Medical Loss Ratio, or MLR, is a prime example of misaligned incentives in the health care supply chain. The Medical Loss Ratio is a provision in the Affordable Care Act that was intended to keep insurance carriers from overcharging their customers. It requires that carriers spend $0.80 of each dollar collected in the small group market, and $0.85 of each dollar collected in the large group market, to pay its customers' medical claims and activities that improve the quality of care. The remaining portion can be used for overhead expenses, such as marketing, profits, salaries, administrative costs, and agent commissions. Once an insurance carrier has achieved every efficiency possible, there is no way to increase profit if health care costs stay the same. If health care costs go up, however, then the carrier is justified in charging higher premiums, thus increasing the value of their 15% or 20%.

Figue 6.1 illustrates what an annual 15% increase in premium (justified by rising health care costs) means to an insurance carrier.

MISALIGNED INCENTIVES:

Figure 6.1

Ok great, what is the alternative? Fortunately, there are a number of effective alternatives to utilize, but let me address the criticisms that will be leveled at those who are looking to jettison the provider network. In addition to the selling point of a sizable discount off of the charges, the other big selling feature of the network is the contractual obligation the provider has to take the agreed upon amount as payment in full. Put another way, the provider can't come after the patient for the difference between what the list price was and the discounted amount. With list prices continuing to rise, there certainly is value in this and folks will argue that without the contractual protections of the network, patients will be at risk of being balance billed. While something to be aware of, there are many different solutions to protect patients from balance billing, so don't let that slow you down. This will be addressed in more detail in relation to specific solutions ahead.

How Many Hospitals Does a Plan Actually Need?

I ask this question in all seriousness, as it is a question that is rarely asked and needs to be asked far more often. The answer to this question will certainly vary from employer to employer, however the conclusion that I believe most will reach is that they have far too many hospitals within their existing network. Have you ever reviewed a report for your plan showing the top ten hospitals used both in terms of actual claims and also dollars spent? If so, you likely saw what most employers see, that after the first 4–5 hospitals, the activity drops significantly for numbers 6–10. Often numbers 8–10 have very few claims, likely related to one-off emergency events. If that is the case, does your plan need access to all 5,534 hospitals in the US? Geography will clearly have the biggest impact on the answer to the question, both in terms of how spread out the population that the plan serves is, but also where the population is located in relation to larger urban areas.

Just using myself as an example, I live near Lake Michigan, meaning that any geographic search for hospitals is limited to 180 degrees, not 360. Within 30 miles of my zip code, there are 7 hospitals, there are 16 within 50 miles, and 97 within 100 miles. Services performed at hospitals can be separated into two categories, emergency and non-emergency, or put another way—elective and otherwise. From an emergency standpoint, time is clearly of the essence and plan participants shouldn't be driving past hospitals to get to one that is covered by the plan. This is why plans today are designed to treat all hospitals as in-network in emergency situations, and I'm not suggesting that this should change. As will be discussed later, the method by which hospitals are reimbursed in these instances should be evaluated, but all hospitals should be an option in emergency situations.

For all other elective/non-emergency situations, however, I personally don't believe I need access to 7 hospitals to choose amongst. This is where the change of mindset needs to come back into play with both employers and employees. If we want to continue to have access to all hospitals all the time, then we need to be prepared to continue to see our costs go up year over year in the form of higher premiums and greater cost sharing when using the plan. With just about everything else that we do in life, we shop around and make informed financial decisions. For example, my wife and I elected to buy plane tickets for spring break where we depart from O'Hare vs. the airport 50 miles from our house. We elected to spend a total of 6 hours in the car with our kids and spend the night in a hotel outside of O'Hare vs. pay 3 times as much for our plane tickets. This concept with regards to health care isn't new. "Consumerism" has been a buzzword in the industry for over 20 years. The fact is, however, that at the individual member level it simply isn't happening in any meaningful way. If it were, costs wouldn't continue to rise year over year. The primary reasons for the failure at the individual level is that (1) individuals either haven't had access to information needed to make an informed decision, or (2) they haven't had enough motivation in the form of an impactful financial incentive, or (3) they don't have the leverage needed to make a dent, or all three.

One of the key foundational items of a Total Control Heath Plan is building a plan that ensures access to the best providers at the best price rather than simply providing access to as many providers as every other plan offers. Will this take work at the outset and continual maintenance? Yes it will, but the long-term financial impact will be well worth the effort.

Direct Contracting

One concept that employers have been using successfully for quite some time is going directly to the source and bypassing the provider network all together. Hospitals and physicians are very open to the idea of establishing a direct contract with employer-sponsored plans. Why would they consider this? For the same reason providers join networks, they are also interested in establishing a relationship directly with an employer if it results in increased patient volume to them. Additionally, as more and more of the liability is shifted to employees through higher deductibles, providers are finding themselves facing a new reality with payments being delayed or neglected entirely. Hospitals know it costs twice as much to collect from an individual rather than an insurance plan. If a provider can secure a direct contract with an employer-sponsored plan, which will likely result in better benefits and reduced liability to the end user, they dramatically reduce the number of people they need to chase for payment as well as reduce the revenue cycle. The beauty of a direct contract with a provider or group of providers is that the plan is now in the driver's seat vs. the carrier/network.

There will be no more guessing as to what you are going to pay for various services. You may find that after reviewing your historical claims utilization that 70% of your claims are going through one particular health care system. If that is the case, wouldn't it make sense to negotiate lower prices in return for rewarding plan participants who use that system with significantly better benefits (i.e., an incentive in the form of lower deductible, etc.).

A word of caution, however, when engaging in direct contracting discussions with providers: Do everything possible to stay away from the percentage discount off of billed charges model. If you don't, you'll only be achieving a bigger percentage off a continually rising number. This doesn't fix the problem.

Direct contract doesn't need to be limited to working with doctors and hospitals. In fact, some of the lowest hanging fruit is related to the ancillary service providers. One of the areas of health care with the greatest price variations is lab work. As outlined in his book, *The Company That Solved Healthcare*, John Torinus outlined how

Serigraph established direct contracts with lab providers and others and eliminated or significantly reduced coverage for other similar providers. While it is true that to have a user-friendly heath insurance plan it has to have sufficient access to providers, it certainly isn't true that every option needs to be on the table. Lab work is one of those items where it doesn't really matter where the specimen goes, so long as the results are accurate and come back quickly. Therefore, why wouldn't an employer consider establishing a relationship that results in lower, predictable costs?

Does this mean that I am suggesting that an employer go out and establish direct contracts with every service provider they may interact with? Certainly that is an option, but it is likely far too complicated and time consuming to consider. So, what is the alternative? First, dissect your claims data to find out where the majority of your claims are being incurred, and look for outliers. If you review your claims associated with lab work, for example, and find that the costs your plan is incurring aren't far off from what you'd likely achieve with a direct contract, then put that one on the shelf. The ROI on time and potential participant disruption isn't there. Second, you don't need to do the work yourself. I, for example, have negotiated direct contracts on behalf of my clients, or there are many other service providers who negotiate direct contracts on behalf of employers as well.

Case Study: Ambulatory Surgery Centers

Ambulatory Surgery Centers, or ASCs, as defined by their national association "are modern health care facilities focused on providing same-day surgical care."[18] There are approximately 5,400 ASCs around the country and the common understanding is that they are far more cost effective locations to have surgeries performed than a hospital. Supporting this understanding is the fact that commercial

---

[18] https://www.ascassociation.org/advancingsurgicalcare/asc/-whatisanasc, accessed June 2018.

insurance carriers often have agreements in place with many ASCs resulting in costs that are 30% to 40% of what would be incurred in a typical hospital setting.

So, employers should encourage all of their plan participants to use an ASC whenever possible, right? Not so fast! As it turns out, in an effort to prevent the loss of important revenue, hospitals have either entered into joint ventures with ASCs or simply created their own. When doing so, the ASC can leverage the hospital contract with the commercial carriers, resulting in costs 3 to 5 times higher than a stand alone ASC. As a result, it is incredibly important for employers to have a clear understanding of the pricing model of any ASCs within their network of preferred providers.

Is there an easy button?

A growing trend among commercial carriers is the promotion of narrow or limited networks. What these are is a flashback to the future, returning to the origins of managed care with more limited networks of providers in return for lower costs. While I am not opposed to the concept, as this is largely what direct contracting is, I offer a word of caution surrounding utilizing a pre-built narrow network and calling it good. While utilizing a narrow network might result in a greater discount, you may not be solving any of the underlying issues that a TCHP is looking to solve.

As outlined in Chapter 2, commercial insurance industry and hospital systems continue to vertically integrate as a method to maximize profit at every level. From a business perspective, it makes complete sense. If you can take in premium dollars from employers/individuals, and then use those dollars to pay your own service providers, you keep it all in the family. This is why carriers large and small are acquiring their own pharmacy benefit managers, labs, physicians, dialysis centers, etc. A simple Google search will quickly return examples of this happening all of the time. Take, for example, the recent news about the planned merger of CVS (PBM) and Aetna (health insurer).

So, while it may seem attractive that a carrier is offering you a greater network discount to use a limited or narrow network or lowering your fully insured premium to do so. In reality, they are simply driving more business to their own providers. Additionally, the narrow network concept is still likely based on the flawed percentage discount off of billed charges model, which won't do anything for costs long term. Just keep in mind that simply because the narrow network is ready to pull off the shelf, there may be better solutions if you go it alone.

Reference Based Pricing

As previously stated, two of the primary flaws of the percentage discount off of charges model is the lack of transparency and the inability of that model to effectively address price. It stands to reason then, that for an alternative to be effective, it must address both of those flaws. If all pricing information were fully transparent, it would likely result in the marketplace quickly reaching equilibrium. Gone would be the days of hospitals five miles apart receiving drastically different payments for the exact same procedure. From a pricing standpoint, if the same information were readily available to both sides in the transaction, we'd find ourselves in a significantly different situation where the customer (i.e., entity paying for the service) would have a much greater influence on price. This would logically lead to a much more efficient market where artificial price increases would cease.

To recap, in order to have an effective alternative to the historical discount of charges model, a new model would need to have a commonly available transparent benchmark available to all participants where the customer has a greater influence over price. If only something like that existed.

Well, fortunately it does.

Medicare (Federal) and Medicaid (State) are the second most common source of health insurance covering 23% of Americans after private health insurance at 56%. As with private health insurance, public health insurance is not immune to rising costs, however the approach the Centers for Medicare and Medicaid Services (CMS) has taken to this challenge has been much different than the private health insurance industry.

Starting with the passage of the Social Security Amendments Act of 1983, Medicare and eventually state Medicaid plans shifted from a retrospective cost basis payment model to a prospective payment system (PPS). Under the retrospective model, "hospitals were paid whatever they spent; there was little incentive to control costs, because higher costs brought about higher levels of reimbursement."[19] As members of the officials and civil servants worked to identify solutions to steadily rising costs, they determined that partly due to the retrospective model and associated incentives to provide more and more services, "hospital costs increased at a rate much higher than the overall rate of inflation."[20]

"Recognizing the inherently inflationary incentives provided by retrospective cost-based reimbursement, the U.S. Congress legislated several interim changes in the Medicare reimbursement system, as part of Public Law 97-248, the Tax Equity and Fiscal Responsibility Act of 1982 (TEFRA). In addition, the Department of Health and Human Services was directed to propose a plan for the prospective payment of hospitals under Medicare that would provide built-in incentives for hospital management efficiency. A report containing such a proposal was delivered to Congress in

---

[19] Stuart Guterman and Allen Dobson, "CMS Special Report," (Spring 1986).
[20] Ibid.

December 1982, and a prospective payment system (PPS) for Medicare inpatient hospital services was legislated in the spring of 1983. Implementation of PPS began on October I, 1983."[21]

The primary objective of the new payment system was to curb the growth in hospital costs, while at the same time allowing for access to high quality health care and fair compensation to hospitals and health care providers. The end result of the changes, the prospective payment system, was "designed to pay a single flat rate per type of discharge, as determined by the classification of each case into a diagnosis-related group (DRG). The DRGs are used to classify patients into groups that are clinically coherent and homogeneous with respect to resource use. Such a classification scheme allows for equitable payment across hospitals in that comparable services can be comparably remunerated. From the prospective of the Medicare program, prospective payment rates have four essential characteristics:

- "They are determined in advance and fixed for the fiscal period to which they apply."
- "The payment rates for any individual hospital are not automatically determined by the level or pattern of its present or past incurred costs or charges."
- "They constitute payment in full for the specific unit of service."
- "Each hospital keeps, or loses, the difference between the payment rate and its costs for that unit of care."[22]

"These characteristics are intended to provide strong financial incentives for hospitals to control their input costs and resource use. Prospective payment thus provides a potential solution to the problem of increasing hospital expenditures that threatens the solvency of the Medicare program. The success or failure of the

---

[21] Ibid.
[22] Ibid.

prospective payment will be determined by its ability to elect a suitable change in the behavior of those who manage the Nation's hospitals."

The information above is from a CMS report reviewing the initial impacts of the change in payment models from 1986, but the last paragraph could have been written a week ago and it would still be relevant.[23]

What is very interesting is that at the same time as the PPS was being introduced, a shift in payment models was also occurring with private health insurance. After the passage of the Social Security Amendment Act of 1983, many observers felt that private health insurance, which was dominated by various Blue Cross Blue Shield entities covering nearly 86 million people in 1982, would also shift to a prospective payment model. Up until that point, while there was no universal payment methodology, the majority of the 75 autonomous BCBS plans used a cost-based reimbursement model, with the remainder using a charge-based model. While a small number of the payers adopted a PPS model or some components of a PPS model like diagnostic-related groups, the majority of BCBS plans were pursuing managed care alternatives. In 1984, there were approximately 2 million members in HMOs and PPOs, and in 2015 there were almost 251 million people enrolled in HMOs (89.1) and PPOs (161.5).[24] This is compared to 55.5 million Medicare enrollees in 2015 and 56.5 million Medicaid enrollees.[25]

---

[23] Ibid.
[24] https://managedcaredigest.com/pdf/HMO-PPO.pdf, accessed June 2018.
[25] https://www.kff.org/medicare/state-indicator/total-medicare-beneficiaries/?currentTimeframe=0&sortModel=%7B%22colId%22:%22Location%22,%22sort%22:%22asc%22%7D, accessed June 2018.

So which approach worked?

Data from KFF Site on Medicare Spending

Over the past 25 years, Medicare spending has grown at a slightly slower rate than private health insurance spending on a per enrollee basis. With the recent slowdown in the growth of Medicare spending, the difference in growth rates between Medicare and private health insurance spending per enrollee widened.

Between 1991 and 2016, Medicare spending per enrollee grew at an average annual rate of 5.0 percent, slower than the 5.7 percent average annual growth rate in private insurance spending per enrollee.

Between 2000 and 2010, per enrollee spending growth rates were comparable for Medicare and private insurance. Between 2010 and 2016, however, Medicare per capita spending grew considerably more slowly than private insurance spending, increasing at an average annual rate of just 1.3 percent over this time period, while average annual private health insurance spending per capita grew at 3.5 percent. It is worth noting that the uptick in private health insurance increases coincided with the passage of the Affordable Care Act with the MLR referenced previously.

In addition to understanding the rate at which costs are increasing each year, it is also very important to understand where the costs are starting from. If both private and public insurance were paying the same thing for each service, the slower rate of inflation experienced by public insurance would be very appealing. But what if the slower rate of inflation was added to lower prices for each service as well? This would be an ideal scenario.

As a point of comparison between the average cost for commercial carriers and Medicare (both traditional Medicare and Medicare

Advantage), a study released by the Congressional Budget Office in June 2017 provides very meaningful insight. The study used 2013 claims data from three large insurers (Aetna, Humana, United Healthcare), normalized it, and compared it to Medicare data.

Study conclusions:
- The average commercial payment rate for a hospital admission in 2013 was about $21,400.
- The average Medicare FFS rate for the same set of stays (in the same hospitals) was about $11,400.
- On average, commercial rates were 89 percent higher than Medicare FFS rates.

Before I dive into what this information means for employers, I'd like to share one unscientific observation, and a few other key pieces of information.

Key Items

There are multiple variations of reimbursement models, both within the PPS model and within PPOs and HMOs. The information I am sharing is intended to provide a broad overview and highlight general trends. The beauty of a Total Control Health Plan is that an employer can determine what model is best for them and proceed down that path.

There is no perfect solution, especially in the scale of both large private and public health insurance plans, which again is why I believe employers are the ideal laboratory to implement different strategies for cost containment.

Unscientific observation: With 56% of the US population covered by private insurance, largely based on a flawed model with disincentives to cost reduction, costs have increased at a far greater rate than would have been experienced with a larger percentage of the population covered by a plan using a prospective payment system.

So what does this mean for employers? As stated at the outset of this section, the two key missing components from the private health insurance market is a commonly available benchmark and a greater influence on price by the customer (rate/claim payer in this case). To address the benchmark piece first, with Medicare being a publicly-funded program, the reimbursement amounts for all services for all hospitals that receive payments from Medicare are publicly available. Additionally, there is absolutely nothing prohibiting any other insurer or plan from using that information to base their own payments off of which brings us to the concept of Reference Based Pricing (RBP). A very simple concept, RBP is the process by which an insurance plan reimburses providers based on a predetermined benchmark, in this case the Medicare fee schedule. For example, rather than the common PPO model where a plan pays X% of Y price, when both X and Y are unknown to the employer, a plan instead pays 1.4 x Medicare for any service where both the multiple and the price are known quantities. This clearly is a far more favorable transaction where both parties clearly understand exactly what is being provided at what price prior to the services being rendered.

As a point of comparison, the Congressional Budget Office study referenced previously outlines where commercial pricing falls as a multiple of Medicare. At the 10th percentile, commercial pricing is 1.44 x Medicare, the 50th percentile is at 1.88 x Medicare, and the 90th percentile is 2.48 x Medicare. Where does your plan fall today? Don't know? You're not alone. What if, however, your plan was designed to pay 1.2 x Medicare, or 1.4 x Medicare, or even 1.5 x Medicare? Depending on your reality today, there could be significant opportunities to not only pay significantly less than you are paying today, but also base those payments on a stable benchmark based in reality. Now we're talking! Why wouldn't a self-insured plan do this? Before I dive into the why and why not, it is important to provide more background on the concept.

First, the most important item to remember if you are considering using a RBP model is that it will be used in conjunction with a Total Control Health Plan. What this means is that the sky is the limit in terms of how and to what extent you use this concept. For example, you could elect to use a RBP reimbursement model for your out-of-network claims only. As the name implies, out-of-network claims are incurred with providers that are outside of the primary network meaning that no network discount applies, or if one does it is through a wrap network or similar service which typically provides a much smaller discount. Rather than facing a small discount of off billed charges, your plan could be designed to pay 1.X of Medicare for out-of-network claims.

As an alternative, you could use RBP for all claims both in- and out-of-network, or you could choose to only use this model for facility claims (hospital, surgery centers, etc.) but use a PPO network for all physician claims. The point is that being a TCHP, the sky is the limit and you can decide what makes the most sense for your plan based on a complete review of the information you now have access to because you have a Total Control Health Plan.

Second, you will not only have control over in what context you use RBP, but you will also have control over what multiple of the benchmark you will use.

So, why not?

Depending on who you ask, you will get a list of reasons why RBP is a "risky" or "bad" idea. I will review some of those reasons in no particular order.

No Contract

The most common objection to using a RBP model is that to do so you are foregoing the security of the network contract. Without it, it will be argued, that every plan participant is at risk of being "balance billed" the difference between what the provider billed and what the plan paid. This is a fair argument, if it were simply left at that, but this is not the case. The facilitation of RBP arrangements is a growing market and the various players in the market take different approaches to mitigating this risk, such as proactively establishing direct contracts with providers for all claims paid by a particular plan.

Litigious

But what happens in the event a contract isn't established before a claim is incurred, and one of your employees receives a balance bill? This is where the RBP administrator earns their keep and ultimately it can be resolved in one of two ways, litigation or negotiation. In the case of litigation, once the administrator is made aware of the balance bill they step in on behalf of the member and start the process of negotiating a settlement with the hospital. Negotiation can go one of two ways, either the administrator will state that the plan isn't budging on the payment (1.2 x Medicare, for example) and they can fight it in court if the hospital doesn't like it, or the administrator can ratchet up the multiple until they hit a point the hospital can live with. As you can imagine, both options have their drawbacks.

I'll take the easy one first. In the case of ratcheting up the multiple of Medicare until an agreement is reached, it is conceivable that the plan may actually end up paying a multiple higher than what it would have achieved through a typical network arrangement. Add to the higher payment the fee paid to the RBP administrator, and the plan is worse off.

With regards to litigation, there isn't anyone who wants to deal with this. While various models exist, a number of the administrators fight on behalf of the member and the plan meaning that neither is exposed to any liability. The downside is that these types of things could drag on for some time, and can become a source of stress for the member. As mentioned previously, the various administrators take different approaches to this issue. Some advocate starting with a higher multiple to begin with, thus reducing the likelihood of a battle but also reducing the potential for savings. Others will start lower and look to fight it. This has a greater potential savings to the plan, but also can get messy. All of them, however, stand by exceptionally high success rates of close to 100% or 100% in terms of favorable resolution. The key takeaway is that as you evaluate RBP for your plan, clearly understand how your administrator plans to handle balance billing situations and explore different options.

Employee Engagement

To make a RBP model work, the plan participants need to be very well educated on this new type of plan structure. Depending on how the plan is designed, the member's ID card may not have the PPO/HMO network logo they have grown accustomed to. This is certainly a benefit in that the member is no longer tied to a particular network of providers, but they may also get pushback from a provider when the logo isn't on the card.

From an advocacy standpoint, the plan participants must be very familiar with what to do in the event they receive a balance bill from a provider. The administrator will not be able to handle the resolution process on behalf of the member if they don't know about the claim.

Medicare Underpays Hospitals

It is a fact that we all want the best health care for ourselves and those that we love, and as we have covered before, that sort of care can be expensive. The question is, how expensive? For the casual observer listening to the news from time to time, it is likely you've heard that Medicare and Medicaid payments don't actually cover the cost of the services rendered. It is also likely that you've heard that "cost shifting" from public insurance to private insurance is part of the reason that costs keep going up. So is it true, and if so, should a private insurance plan base reimbursement off of the Medicare fee schedule?

According to a report released by the American Hospital Association in December 2017, across their membership on average Medicare reimbursed hospitals for $0.87 of every dollar spent and Medicaid reimbursed hospitals $0.88 for every dollar spent. Additionally, 66% of hospitals received payments less than cost from Medicare and 61% received payments less than cost from Medicaid.

To address this issue, many RBP administrators reimburse hospitals in one of two ways. The first is the already discussed multiple of Medicare model. The alternative is reimbursing a multiple actual cost, whichever is higher. The good news is that hospitals have to report actual costs for services Medicare provided as reviewed prior (Stanford). As the argument goes, if a plan is willing to pay 1.2 or 1.4 times the actual cost of the service, as reported to Medicare by the hospital, there shouldn't be a problem.

Departure from the Norm

For the majority of employees covered by an employer-sponsored plan today, the use of a provider network is all they have ever known. The idea of no longer using a hospital network could be disconcerting to employees if it isn't communicated well. Frankly for me, I don't believe this should be a roadblock. Remember, if you keep doing what you've always done…

Too Much Work, Not Enough Reward

As outlined in the CBO analysis comparing Medicare pricing to commercial insurance, the variability between the two varies significantly based on geography. In some areas of the country it is common for billed charges to exceed 10 x Medicare, where in others the differential is less than 3. The point is, that in order to determine if RBP is a model that will work for your plan, you first need to determine where you are starting from with the networks at your disposal. If the network discount results in pricing to the plan that isn't significantly higher than what you might experience using RBP, then you may elect to focus on other means to reduce your costs first.

Case Study: ClaimDOC

In 2012, a trucking company based in Southern California received yet another double-digit increase to their fully-insured plan. With just over 800 employees on the plan, they were looking at a $4.5 million expense. Fast forward to 2013, with the same headcount, they were given a 15% increase to their plan. Seeing a non-sustainable trend and facing a $5 million expense, the executive team was getting worried. In 2014, their carrier offered their best renewal: a 25% increase. Over $6.2 million. More than double the expense since 2011 despite having the same number of employees.

It was time for a change. Enter ClaimDOC. That year the plan elected to implement a self-insured plan with an independent TPA and utilize ClaimDOC's RBP model. At the close of the year, the plan slowly added additional employees and finished the year at

$5.4 million—over $800,000 below the fully-insured quote. In 2015, their headcount jumped to an average of 934 and expenses held at $6.4 million. In 2016, they added another 130 employees and cut costs to just over $5 million. In 2017, they saw another 100 jobs added with costs at $6.1 million, the approximate expense they expected in 2014 with 350 fewer positions!

By implementing ClaimDOC, a company in a low-margin, highly competitive environment was able to steadily hire significantly more drivers with no change in turnover ratio, and flatten their health care spend. Had the group stayed fully-insured, and estimating the lowest annual premium increase they had received in the prior five years (10%), the plan cost could have reached $11.3 million. With ClaimDOC's program expertise, their plan spend is now half of that figure and holding flat.

Conclusions

From my perspective, the days of the provider network as we know it today are limited. The lack of transparency and the incentives to continue rising prices will not be tolerated much longer, in fact many employers have already said "enough." As always, change is difficult and it requires effort but the end result for employers who have elected to challenge the status quo is a far more appealing and sustainable reality. Not only are their costs going down due to reasonable and predictable pricing, but their stop loss carriers are rewarding them with lower premiums as well. Implementing strategies such as direct contracting, reference based pricing, and others are examples of employers taking control over their health care supply chain. It can and must be done in order to change the status quo.

Chapter 7
Pharmacy Benefit Managers

When writing a book about health insurance costs and the health care supply chain, the cost of prescription drugs certainly needs to be addressed. The challenge, however, is that entire books have been written about this topic alone, as there is no more complicated and murky aspect of the health care supply chain than the prescription drug component of it. Just as with the lack of transparency within the provider networks, the prescription drug supply chain is full of players with little incentive to actually reduce costs, and every player blames the other for rising costs. Therefore, my goal with this chapter is to provide the reader with a good understanding of the basic components of the prescription supply chain and where employer profit is sucked out of the plan. Additionally, I will provide insight into some of the most common pitfalls to avoid when seeking to take control over your prescription supply chain.

Unlike the medical side of the health care supply chain, the prescription side is far more difficult to manage for the following reason. With medical claims there are many different providers available for members to seek services from and for health plans to negotiate with. Brand name and specialty prescription drugs, on the other hand, originate with a single manufacturer, which makes negotiation far more difficult. The idea of a single employer negotiating with every pharmaceutical manufacturer to establish the best pricing possible is simply unrealistic. As a result, this role has been filled by the Pharmacy Benefit Manager (PBM), which is an industry that has evolved from relative obscurity, as recently as the early 1980s, to one that generates hundreds of billions of dollars a year today. The role of the Pharmacy Benefit Manager (PBM), much like the provider network, is a good one in theory. PBMs work on behalf of health plans, negotiating lower prices on the prescription drugs covered by the plan. According to their industry association, PCMA, PBMs will save health plans $2 trillion from 2012 to 2021.

Today, in the United States, there are over 100 PBMs, however the market is largely dominated by the big three: Caremark, Express Scripts, and OptumRx who control over 70% of the market. It is worth noting that OptumRx is owned by United Healthcare, the largest private insurer in the country, and Caremark is pursuing a merger with Aetna, the number three private health insurer. Number 2, Anthem, is currently in the midst of a $15 billion lawsuit with Express Scripts, who they accuse of overcharging them by $3 billion annually. As a result, they are moving forward with plans to establish their own PBM by 2020. In 2016, two-thirds of CVS Caremark's revenue came from their PBM, and one-third of UHC's revenue came from OptumRx. Needless to say, there is big money to be made as a middleman in the prescription supply chain and many players are cashing in.

The reason that any discussion about health insurance costs must include a discussion about prescription drugs is that the fastest growing cost driver for any medical plan is the pharmacy benefit as a percentage of overall costs, at least that is what we've been told repeatedly by health plans each year when the rates go up. But, if you ask the nation's largest Pharmacy Benefits Manager, Express Scripts, they'd argue that prescription costs increased only 1.5% for commercial plans in 2017. Thanks to their efforts, cost are on a downward trend. So, which is it? Well, depending on which piece of the convoluted supply chain you look at, the answer is both.

Manufacturers will argue that while the list price of their drugs may have increased significantly, the net increase has been much smaller due to rebates and other incentives that are given to the PBMs for favorable placement on their respective formularies (i.e., list of approved drugs). From the perspective of the manufacturer, it isn't their fault that PBMs and insurance carriers retain these incentives resulting in rate payers and end users footing the ever increasing bill. PBMs, on the other hand, will argue the opposite pointing to manufacturers and pharmacies, among others, as the reason that costs are going up.

Most readers will recall the furor in 2016 over the 400%+ increase to the price of the Epipen in less than three years. The most offensive example, but certainly not an anomaly, was what the CEO of Turing Pharmaceuticals did when they raised the price of the 60-year-old drug Daraprim by 5500% in 2015 from $13.50 to $750 per pill. As with anything, the truth is somewhere in the middle. In this case, the truth really hurts because while those at the upper end of the supply chain rake in massive profits, those at the bottom are nearing the limits of their ability to pay. This raises the question then, why are manufacturers raising prices and PBMs and carriers retaining larger shares of the rebates? The answer is simple, because they can.

The prescription supply chain is built on confidential agreements between PBMs and manufacturers and between PBMs and carriers, which include no incentives to reduce cost. Employers must seek to understand all of the details of their contracts so that they can take every step possible to keep costs under control. Alex Azar, who became the Secretary of Health and Human Services in 2018 and was the President of Lilly USA, LLC the largest division of Eli Lilly and Company, outlined the broken system to an audience at the Manhattan Institute in 2016.

So about 25 years ago we fell into a system of pharmaceutical rebates which worked fine, so long as insurance plans exposed patients to only limited cost sharing. Drug companies would settle this price for a medicine and they'd sell it to pharmacies at that price. After a pharmacy dispensed that drug to the patient, collecting a modest copay, the patient's insurer or pharmacy benefit manager that the insurer hired would pay the balance of the list price to the pharmacy. The insurer, or the pharmacy benefit manager, would send proof of that payment to the drug company, which would then send a rebate check of 5% or 10%, maybe even 20%, back to the insurer or the PBM. Drug companies offered these rebates so that insurance plans would make their medicines more accessible to patients. A larger rebate usually secured you a better placement on the insurer's or PBM's formulary, which meant patients pay less out-of-pocket for your drugs. The terminology was called "buying down the copay."

The only problem is that nearly every player in the industry—and this is not to fault any player in the industry, it's simply a statement of the economic facts. All players, wholesalers like McKesson and Cardinal, pharmacies like CVS and Walgreens, pharmacy benefit managers like Express Scripts and CVS Caremark, and drug companies, make more money when list prices increase. The fees that middlemen in this channel charge are based on a percentage of list price. So higher list prices generate more fees. If drug companies set their list prices higher, they have more room to offer larger rebates, to win better formulary placement from insurers and PBMs. It's those list prices that have generated all of the recent controversy.

You've heard that drug prices increased each of the past two years by 12 and 13%. Those are like talking about rack rates on the back of your hotel room door. I mean take a look at it the next time you stay at a hotel. It's probably 500, 600, $1,000 more than what you're actually paying for that room, thank goodness. It's the same *with drug prices. Net prices, after drug companies doled out more than 130 billion dollars in rebates, grew just 2.8% last year. They've been growing fairly modestly for several years now, as drug companies raise their rebates nearly as fast as they've been raising list prices.*

No patient was ever supposed to pay those list prices but in recent years a growing number have been forced to do exactly that. Why? Because of big changes in how health insurance benefits are designed.[26]

And there you have it. A supply chain that benefits as price goes up with the rate payers and end users left holding the bag. From my perspective, an even bigger issue than the disincentives to reduce costs built into the supply chain, is the overall complexity and opacity of the system. It includes dozens of terms, like Average Wholesale Price, that mean different things to different people, and shell games are a regular occurrence. For example, I recently reviewed a PBM proposal that had 12 different administrative fees included in it, 12. It doesn't need to be this complicated, there simply isn't a good reason for it other than to provide more moving pieces to hide revenue in.

Before we dive into some of the games PBMs can play, it is first important to better understand that not all PBMs are created equal. PBMs usually operate under one of three different models:
1. Traditional: In a traditional model, a PBM makes money in two primary ways. First, they retain 25% to 50% of all rebates received from the pharmaceutical manufacturers. Second, they make money on "spread" pricing where they sell the drug to the pharmacy and plan for more than they pay for it. For example, if a drug cost $150 and they

---

[26] https://www.manhattan-institute.org/sites/default/files/MI_Azar_Transcript_1116.pdf, accessed June 2018.

obtained it for $96, they'd sell it to the pharmacy for $100, which would then be paid for either by the member, the plan, or both. Typically, they make approximately 2% to 4% spread on brand name medications, and 10% to 20% on generic medications.

2. Pass-through: With a pass-through model, a PBM makes money in two ways again, but they are slightly different. First, like the traditional model they retain a portion of the rebates, but in this case it typically ranges from 5% to 25%. Second, rather than making money on spread, they are compensated by charging an administrative fee that is commonly charged per prescription filled.

3. Fully-transparent: Finally, a fully transparent PBM retains none of the rebates nor do they use spread pricing. Transparent PBMs are simply paid an administrative fee per prescription claim paid. Like everything else in this supply chain, the term "transparent" is used to describe many different PBMs who have different structures and not all of them fully disclose every revenue source. For the purposes of our discussion, let's consider a fully-transparent PBM to be one which will openly and honestly answer the following simple questions:
   - How much in total are you earning from our group?
   - Where is it coming from?
   - Will you make it easy for me to audit our plan?

Now that we established that PBMs come in different shapes and sizes, let's review why it is so important for employers to dive into their specific PBM contract to understand what it actually says. Henry Eickelberg, Managing Director of the Terry Group and a former Fortune 100 corporate executive, wrote a paper for the American Health Policy Institute in December of 2015 that did a fantastic job outlining the uphill battle that employers face when working to manage their prescription supply chain. The following is an excerpt from his paper, which drives the point home:

When it comes to managing the prescription drug supply chain, even the most sophisticated plan sponsors find themselves at a disadvantage to PBMs because only the PBM understands the whole range of the financial opportunities available in the supply chain. The frequent answer for most plan sponsors is to simply re-compete their PBM services, but even with the smoothest of implementations, there is a significant risk of employee disruption when a plan sponsor moves from one PBM to another. This fact gives plan sponsors great pause when considering their options.

As a general rule, PBMs tend to be very tough negotiators and with good reason. PBMs possess superior knowledge of the prescription drug supply chain. PBMs understand and can better anticipate future changes in the marketplace. In the end, PBM contracts tend to be very one-sided and often include:

- *Sharp limitations on client access to data (even claims data that documents what the PBM is asking the plan sponsor to reimburse);*
- *Unclear or heavily ambiguous definitions (or even silence) for important terms;*
- *Sharp limits on audit rights and stringent approval process for audit firms (including excluding some audit firms from the ability to act on behalf of a client);*
- *A lack of clarity in the PBM's drug pricing algorithm;*
- *A lack of transparency in the PBM's retail network contracts (most plan sponsors do not realize that a PBM may have multiple contracts with the exact same retail network);*
- *A lack of disclosure as to the financial incentives the PBM may receive from manufacturers and/or wholesalers;*
- *Pricing disparities between retail dispensed drugs and the cost of the same drug dispensed by the PBM's mail order facility;*
- *Definitional issues between generic verses brand drugs; and*

- *A habit of directing patients to higher cost therapies just prior to the therapy losing patent protection.*

While there are additional areas that a plan sponsor needs to concern itself with in PBM contracting, the above list gives a flavor for the sophistication needed when contracting with and effectively monitoring a PBM. Further exacerbating this situation is the fact that benefit consulting firms hired to assist plan sponsors have worked out less than transparent 'deals' with specific PBMs. These deals between the consultant and the PBM significantly call into question the consultant's independence.

Below are some examples of challenges that plan sponsors face when contracting with a PBM:

Package Size Pricing: *Typically, a PBM promises a plan sponsor a certain percentage discount to the Average Wholesale Price (AWP); e.g., 16 percent off AWP for brand named drugs. What is not readily apparent is that the AWP price is based heavily on the package size. For example, the plan sponsor's price guarantee may be measured as some percentage discount off of AWP for a package size of 100 pills (or in some cases, less), whereas the PBM is likely purchasing the drug in lots of 50,000 or greater at a substantially lower price point. Structuring the PBM contract in this manner (which is often silent) allows the PBM to say it saved the plan sponsor some percentage off of AWP, when in fact the actual drug acquisition cost as to the PBM was significantly less.*

Retail Network Management: *In addition to mail-order pharmacy services, PBMs contract with broad retail networks. What is not apparent to most plan sponsors (or their consultants) is that the PBM will often have multiple contracts (with varying financial arrangements) with the exact same retail pharmacy networks. So plan sponsors believing that they have secured a fully-transparent PBM contract may well be subsidizing a separate contract as* *previously stated.* The question then arises as to what would drive a PBM to act in this manner? Again, the reason is that the PBM is trying to manage its aggregate contractual relationship with the retailer to make sure that PBM is delivering on its financial commitments to the retail chain. In doing this, some plan sponsors win, while others lose. Who wins and who loses is typically based on the bargaining power with small and medium size companies (and multi-employer health & welfare funds) paying substantially more. All PBM clients do not get the same economic advantage with bigger clients getting bigger (better) deals and smaller clients get smaller (less lucrative) deals – said differently, the size of the relationship does matter.

PBM Formulary Management: PBMs have an incentive to tightly manage their formularies. As such, it would not be unusual for a PBM to reshuffle their formulary within a year of an important drug losing its patent protection. The PBM would do this to continue to secure rebate dollars from the manufacturers. For example, within a year of Lipitor losing patent protection, it would not be unheard of for a PBM to change its formulary to remove Lipitor as the designated brand-name drug for that therapeutic class and replace it with Crestor, which was not losing patent protection for some time. By doing so, the PBM can maintain its rebate dollars from Crestor's manufacturer.

Inability to Access Claims Data: Plan sponsors who want to bid their PBM contracts have frequently found out that their current PBM will not give the plan sponsor their own data necessary to bid out the PBM contract. PBMs frequently refuse to turnover this information citing various privacy and contractual constraints. (Authors note: One technique for motivating PBM's to comply with data requests is to tell them if they are unwilling to release the information, the employer will require the PBM to take a co-fiduciary status as a condition of retaining the business. This commonly moves things along more quickly.)

Auditor Selection and Approval: *Understandably, PBMs jealously guard their propriety information. PBM contracts often give the PBM the right to veto the plan sponsor's choice of auditor assigned to validate the financial guarantees embedded in a PBM contract. In addition, PBM contracts often limit the length of time the plan sponsor has the right to audit (the audit can only look back over the last two years).*

PBM Pricing Algorithms: *PBMs use complex pricing algorithms to derive the plan sponsor's 'cost' or to show that the PBM met an agreed-to price guarantees. For example, the PBM may guarantee that the plan sponsor will not pay any more than AWP minus 16 percent. The percentage savings (16 percent) is determined by dividing the total ingredient costs for all drugs purchased by the total AWP for all drugs purchased. Achievement of this savings target is determined on an aggregate basis. If the savings the PBM promised are not achieved, the PBM will pay the plan sponsor the difference. However, in determining whether the percentage off of AWP was actually achieved, some PBMs will exclude certain claim types from the calculation that would hurt the PBMs performance and include others that alter the performance calculation. In addition, some PBMs may use an artificially low ingredient cost that allows them to achieve the aggregate savings guarantee. For example, in cases where the plan sponsor pays the entire cost of the drug (because the cost of the drug is less than the employee's copay), the PBM may stick in a minimal cost figure (e.g., $0.05) for the ingredient cost to allow the PBM to book a large discount to the AWP.*

Contractual Over-Charging: *There have been some instances of PBMs deliberately failing to meet contractually-required price guarantees by over-charging the employer more money throughout the year. When the guarantee calculation is processed after the close of the year, it turns out that the PBM owes the plan sponsor a sizable refund. By over-charging the plan sponsor throughout the* *year and settling up some time after the year has closed, the PBM is essentially using the plan sponsor's capital at no cost. If in response, a frustrated plan sponsor decides to bid out the work, the plan sponsor may put any pending refunds at-risk. During the PBM bidding process, the current PBM may suspend processing further refunds pending the bidding process outcome, and pocket the guarantee money if the incumbent PBM loses the work.*

Rebates versus Purchase Order Discounts: *PBMs are paid rebates because the PBMs run clinical programs that steer employees to certain medications. Given the fact that many plan sponsors understand that the PBM is securing rebates, plan sponsors have asked the PBM for 'transparent' pricing. If in response, the industry has moved to 'reclassifying' the rebate dollars as "purchase order discounts' or 'administrative fees'. Since the plan sponsor is often only contractually entitled to those things specifically defined in the contract as a "rebate," the PBM will pocket the purchase order discounts. Thus, while a plan sponsor may believe that it has negotiated a fully 'transparent' PBM deal (receiving 100 percent of the revenue coming from the manufacturer), what the plan sponsor doesn't realize is that some portion of the rebates have been carved-off and paid to the PBM as a purchase order discounts or admin fee etc.*

Definitions – Brand versus Generic: *The way a drug is defined (i.e., whether generic vs. brand) drives which aggregate discount the drug contributes to (i.e., the generic discount or the brand discount). PBMs use the contract language to exercise great discretion in determining when a drug has actually moved from 'brand' to 'generic.' The timing may have a great impact on the pricing guarantees the PBM has contractually obligated itself to supply. For example, even after a drug has a generic equivalent available, PBMs may not consider the drug as a generic (and include in the drug in the generic pricing guarantees) until the PBM has determined (in its sole discretion) that there is a* sufficient supply in the marketplace, which could be months or years after the drug has gone generic.

Reimbursements Differences Between Retail and Mail-Order: *It is not unusual to find a PBM reimbursing a retail pharmacy network less than the cost the plan sponsor is being charged for the same drug through the PBM's mail order service (i.e., spread pricing). This fact was the primary motivation for the creation of the HR Policy Association's PharmaDirect program.*

Manufacturer Administrative Fees: *In the PBM/Manufacturer contract, the PBM will require that the manufacturer pay the PBM an 'administrative' fee. The PBM will not classify these funds as a 'rebate.' The payment is to offset the PBM's costs in reporting drug usage data back to the manufacturer so that the manufacturer can calculate any rebate due the PBM, as well as better understand the market data for its drugs.*

Mail-Order Purchase Discount: *Finally, a fairly recent scheme now being deployed is the use of a "mail-order purchase discount.' The drug manufacturer pays these funds to the PBM for drugs dispensed through the PBM's mail order facility (as well as any PBM owned retailed pharmacies). In the vast majority of plan sponsor/PBM contracts, the PBM is retaining 100 percent of these funds claiming that they are not a manufacturer's rebate as defined by the plan sponsor's contract with the PBM.*[27]

So, what is an employer to do? With the cost of prescription drugs increasing at a much higher rate than medical claims, it won't be long before prescription claims represent 50% of your cost and therefore it is incredibly important to have a working knowledge of your prescription supply chain. As discussed throughout this book,

---

[27] http://www.americanhealthpolicy.org/Content/documents/resources/December%202015_AHPI%20Study_Understanding_the_Pharma_Black_Box.pdf, accessed June 2018.

if your plan is fully insured today, there isn't much you can do to address the structure of the PBM contract your carrier has implemented. If your plan is self-insured with a carrier or a carrier-owned TPA, it is also highly unlikely you will be able to impact pricing in a significant way. In fact, in many cases a portion of the rebates secured by the PBM is passed along to the carrier, which becomes a significant source of income.

Ultimately there are more than 15 different sources of revenue for a PBM, and in many cases it is extremely hard to identify them all. With the largest PBMs being publicly-traded companies or owned by publicly-traded companies, you can be sure that a CEO is not going to willingly reduce his/her profitability. As a result, without full transparency, you may believe you have secured more favorable contract terms through negotiation but in reality, like squeezing a water balloon, the reduction in one revenue stream is compensated for with an increase in another.

After getting to this point, you are likely thinking that it is an absolute no-brainer to move to a transparent PBM. While that may be true, unfortunately it isn't quite as simple as that. For example, as outlined previously, the big three PBMs have significantly more market clout than a smaller start-up transparent PBM. The big three will argue that their bargaining power will result in better discounts than the transparent PBMs are able to provide. That being said, personally I don't believe a relationship where one party willingly withholds information from another is a relationship that I want to have. As a result, I believe employers should strongly consider working with a fully transparent PBM. Again, for the purposes of our discussion, a fully transparent PBM is one who will answer the following questions:
- How much in total are you earning from our group?
- Where is it coming from?
- Will you make it easy for me to audit our plan?

Here is the good news, unlike the complexity and cost associated with a re-pricing analysis for medical claims, assuming you can get your Rx data and existing contract, a re-pricing analysis for prescriptions is much easier, relatively speaking. Through a re-pricing analysis, an employer will be able to determine if an alternative PBM is able to provide greater discounts on the same prescriptions. As with everything tied to prescriptions, games can be played with the re-pricing and RFP process as well. It is very important to ensure that when requesting a RFP from alternative PBMs, that an apples-to-apples formulary comparison is done. It isn't uncommon for PBMs to swap out drugs on the formulary for others that they may secure greater rebates from, but also that might cost the plan more. If an employer is solely focused on rebates, this will be very attractive, but from a net cost standpoint the employer actually loses.

Case Study: Performance Pharmacy Solutions

Performance Pharmacy Solutions (PPS) is "a unique pharmacy resource developed to efficiently and effectively evaluate, manage, and oversee your self-funded client's pharmacy benefit management programs" based in Massachusetts.[28] PPS has worked to develop contracts with four of the largest PBMs in the country, and provides proposals to self-funded employers from all four players to quickly and easily provide competitive bids. Importantly, their model is based on providing full transparency to the plan sponsors so that it is clear where all dollars are flowing.

Since their founding in 2012, PPS has grown steadily by taking business from many of the largest commercial carriers, who use the same PBMs! When I first learned about PPS, I questioned how they would be able to negotiate better contracts and bigger discounts than the large commercial carriers who cover significantly more people. Their response was very insightful, "we

---

[28] https://get-pps.com/about/, accessed June 2018.

can't, that's the point." While PPS isn't able to negotiate as big a discount as a big commercial carrier may be able to with the same PBM, the net result to the client is better because PPS does not retain anything for themselves while carriers often don't pass the same discount they achieve from the PBM on to their clients. Here is a simple illustration to make the point.

The following are the results of recent contract comparisons that PPS completed for prospective clients:

- Group has 1,388 lives, a large national commercial carrier was the incumbent using Express Scripts, moving to a PPS contract with Express Scripts generated an annual savings projection of $437,868.00.
- Group has 2,100 lives, a large publicly-traded commercial carrier was the incumbent, moving to a PPS contract with Express Scripts generated an annual savings projection of $820,211.00.
- Group has 420 lives, a regional commercial carrier was the incumbent using Express Scripts, moving to a PPS contract with Express Scripts generated an annual savings projection of $36,252.20.

As important as establishing favorable contractual terms on the front end, is monitoring the execution of the terms on an ongoing basis. PPS provides semi-annual contract compliance reviews to ensure that the pricing that was promised, is delivered.

Case Study: Truveris

Truveris, a start-up tech company, has built a new platform that significantly streamlines the PBM RFP process, as well as, provides a web-based dashboard that is available to employer customers for real time monitoring of contractual compliance.

More than 300 employers ranging from small- to medium-sized businesses and local labor unions to large, multi-national corporations with more than 50,000 employees are saving money through the Truveris TruBid platform. Truveris technology has helped negotiate coverage for nearly 7 million people and has influenced more than $9 billion of pharmaceutical spend.

The outcome of a contract between Truveris and the State of New Jersey to assist with reducing the state's prescription drug spend will result in a savings of approximately 18% on a new three-year contract with OptumRx.

New Jersey becomes the first state government to use Truveris' technology platform across multiple-employee populations. The cooperation between the legislature, unions, and the state on behalf of the taxpayers of New Jersey was essential in opening up an enormous opportunity for cost savings on the prescription drug program.

The state has historically spent approximately $2.2 billion annually to provide prescription drug benefits to employees, dependents, and retirees of the School Employee's Health Benefits Plan, the State Health Benefits Plan, and the Employer Group Waiver Plans (EGWP).

The new contract will result in a total three-year savings of nearly $1.6 billion. To achieve this, Truveris helped the state conduct a reverse auction that included three pharmacy benefits managers (PBMs). In the reverse auction, the bidders were provided with historical data on nearly 11 million prescriptions that were covered by the state in 2016. During two rounds of blind bidding, the PBMs offered their best prices for the state's three-year contract. The Truveris technology platform priced the proposals utilizing code-based classification of drugs from nationally-accepted data sources.

Traditionally, the vendor selection process can take more than six months. By leveraging Truveris' technology platform, the state concluded the entire process in less than two months.

Ongoing Bill Review Helps Ensure Compliance

After the new contract is implemented, Truveris will apply its ongoing bill review solution for the first year of the contract to help ensure that OptumRx is delivering on its contractual commitments to the state.

Bill review is the first independent claims adjudication platform to validate and ensure financial accuracy based on contract terms and definitions, of 100% of pharmacy claims on a vendor's invoice. All the reporting and analytic features are delivered through a secure portal which has the capacity to receive and process all pharmacy data and re-adjudicate each individual claim to identify contract variance instantaneously.

Specialty drugs: A small, but very important subset of prescription drugs are those that are deemed "specialty," and like many other terms in the prescription supply chain, it can be used to mean different things. The American Pharmacy Association defines specialty pharmacy this way, *"Specialty pharmacy focuses on high cost, high touch medication therapy for patients with complex disease states. Medications in specialty pharmacy range from oral to cutting edge injectable and biologic products. The disease states treated range from cancer, multiple sclerosis and rheumatoid arthritis to rare genetic conditions."*[29]

Prices for specialty medications can range from thousands, to tens of thousands, to hundreds of thousands of dollars per year. A 2017

---

[29] https://www.pharmacist.com/specialty-pharmacy, accessed June 2018.

report by Segal Consulting found that specialty medications are projected to increase in cost by 17.7% in 2018, a slight reduction from the 18.7% in 2017. Additionally, they found that specialty drugs accounted for more than one-third of total drug spending in 2016, and they are anticipated to represent 50% of prescription spending by 2020. A further subset of specialty medications is "orphan drugs" which are drugs that are targeted at a patient population of 200,000 or less. As an incentive to pharmaceutical manufacturers to develop treatments for rare diseases with a limited commercial market, the Orphan Drug Act of 1983 was passed giving manufacturers 7-year market exclusivity, fast track approval status, and a number of other perks. In an effort to increase profits, a trend has been developing over the last decade where pharmaceutical manufacturers are focusing their attention on specialty and orphan drugs due to their significant financial windfall if approved.

According to Diplomat, America's largest independent provider of specialty pharmacy services, approximately half of the 22 novel new drugs approved in 2016 were considered specialty drugs, which is a similar proportion to 2015. Eighty-two percent received a special FDA designation (i.e., Breakthrough, Fast Track, Orphan, Accelerated Approval, Priority Review).

I reference this information because it is becoming more and more likely that some of the largest claims a plan faces will not be traditional medical claims, but rather specialty pharmacy claims. It is imperative that employers have a plan to manage these claims as effectively as possible. In an effort to cash in on the explosion in specialty pharmacy claims, the big three PBMs all now have their own specialty pharmacies and often dictate that customers use these pharmacies. While it is important to aggressively manage the source of specialty medications, typically using only one vendor, it is equally important to ensure that the ultimate source you select has incentives in alignment with those of your plan.

As an example, the world's top-selling specialty medication currently is Humira, which is used to treat Rheumatoid Arthritis (RA) among other auto-immune diseases. Humira was evaluated by five different randomized tests, and in one test including 544 patients, participants were given doses of Humira weekly, every other week, or a placebo. Of the patients receiving doses every other week, 46% had a favorable result, while of those receiving doses weekly, 53% had a favorable result compared to 19% of those who received the placebo. Certainly the results are favorable for those who suffer from RA, but when looking at the numbers a different way you could determine that 54% of the population in one case and 47% in the other did not have a favorable outcome. With an annual cost exceeding $60,000, an employer will want to be certain that the specialty pharmacy vendor they are working with has the ability to measure and manage the clinical effectiveness of medications such as Humira that each patient is using. PBMs who own their own specialty pharmacy benefit each time a claim is processed and therefore do not have much of an incentive to identify patients who could benefit from an alternative treatment.

Case Study: VIVIO Health

VIVIO Health is a new specialty drug carve out plan that uses data and analytics to reinvent the use and purchase of specialty drugs. Its products help patients get the right medicine based on their unique health data and disease progression using a continuously improving dataset of real world drug outcomes. VIVIO Health's clinical models typically save employers 20–30% while significantly improving outcomes and member experience.

The CHG family of companies is one of the largest providers of health care staffing in the country. CHG is the leading supplier of locum tenens and also offers both temporary and permanent placement of physicians, nurses, and other health care professionals. Headquartered in Salt Lake City, CHG employs more than 3,750 employees (8,000 members) who are served by three health plans. CHG has made Fortune's list of best places to work for the past eight years.

Like most employers, CHG is wrestling with more employees using specialty drugs and the associated rise in costs. CHG's benefits team spoke with peers and quickly discovered most companies face similar challenges, but none had found an effective solution from existing vendors. CHG's core value of putting people first encourages new vendors to offer better services and member experiences and has resulted in their consistent ranking as a Fortune 100 Best Company to Work For.

CHG's Vice President, Talent Management, Nicole Thurman, identified VIVIO Health as a new and innovative solution for specialty drug management and cost control. CHG purchased VIVIO Precision Care^{TM} program carving out specialty drugs from traditional carriers and PBMs. VIVIO Health successfully integrated its product within CHG's ecosystem of carriers, TPAs, and PBMs.

Results:
- Members paid $0 for specialty medications
- 56% reduction in specialty medication costs through the first 9 months of implementation
- 194% ROI 24 weeks after launch
- 454% ROI 9 months after launch

Likely, the least transparent component of a health insurance plan is the pharmacy benefit. The liability generated by this benefit is representing a larger and larger portion of total plan costs each year. While there are many hurdles placed in front of an employer who is seeking to control this liability, it can and is being done today. From a low-hanging fruit standpoint, with the right advisor it will not be an insurmountable challenge for an employer to achieve full transparency and reduced costs by partnering with like-minded, independent vendors.

Chapter 8
Innovation

So in what other ways is a TCHP different from what you have now? Before I go further, take a moment and think about the most recent innovation you implemented within your business. Maybe it was a new marketing strategy, or a more efficient way of getting goods from point A to point B. Now, do the same exercise but with regard to your health insurance plan. What was the most recent innovation you implemented with regards to your health insurance plan? If your reality is like those who responded to the *SHRM Survey Findings: 2016 Strategic Benefits—Health Care,* you did things like:

- Offered consumer-directed health plans
- Created an organizational culture that promotes health and wellness
- Offered a variety of PPO plans, including those with high and low deductibles
- Increased the employee share contributed to the total costs of health care
- Offered a HMO plan
- Provided incentives or rewards related to health and wellness
- Placed limits on, or increased cost-sharing for spousal health coverage
- Increased the employee share contributed towards the cost of brand name prescription drugs

What was the ROI you received from your most recent business innovation? I'll bet you know the answer to that question.

What was the ROI you received from your most recent health plan innovation? I suspect you are not sure or are struggling to come up with a true ROI. Did it bend your cost curve in the other direction, permanently? Take a second look at the list of actions employers took to address rising health care costs and pick the one that effectively addressed price anywhere within the health care supply chain. Can't find it? That's because it isn't there. The closest you could come would be offering a consumer-driven health insurance plan because in theory they encourage people to shop around, but studies have now shown that doesn't happen. The other disheartening thing is that the list of strategies used by employers as tracked by the annual SHRM survey hasn't changed for at least 5 years.

"Dang, it hurts when I hit myself with this hammer!"

"Then stop hitting yourself with the hammer!"

If we think back to what PWC outlined in their trend projections referenced earlier, "heading into 2018, employers should look to new contract arrangements with providers to tackle healthcare prices without shifting more costs to employees" none of the strategies that employers commonly use today will do that.[30]

This is the issue, and while innovation happens all around us, every day in business, the commercial health insurance industry has been largely devoid of meaningful innovation. Why? Because they are simply too vested in the status quo. That being said, there are hundreds of small innovative companies that are working

---

[30] https://www.pwc.com/us/en/health-industries/health-research-institute/behind-the-numbers/reports/hri-behind-the-numbers-2018.pdf, accessed June 2018.

successfully and feverishly to disrupt the health insurance market. So why haven't you heard about them? The reality is that if your health insurance plan today is not self-insured with an independent TPA, your group is being lumped in with every other employer in a one size fits all box. It simply isn't practical for a health insurance carrier to have more than one service provider in each category. Sure, your carrier likely has a strong marketing department and you are seeing new and flashy things at each renewal, but if we are honest with each other—what meaningful innovation have you been presented that actually reduced your costs sustainably without shifting cost to the end user?

The reality is that you need to think of your health insurance plan as a start up and run it that way. You now know that you have a health insurance business and the competition (i.e., cost) is trying to eat you alive. You need to be prepared to try new things and embrace failure, but you need to fail fast. As I mentioned earlier in the book, I was fortunate to be invited to join a peer group of the top independent thought leaders in employee benefits throughout the country—the NextGen Benefits Mastermind Partnership. We meet quarterly and share the latest ideas, solutions, and vendors we are seeing help bend the cost curve down. New innovation comes up in every meeting. Innovation is happening in health insurance and disruption is happening, so why isn't it happening with your plan? Not every solution you try will be a home run, but with solid information and the flexibility to try new things, you will certainly be hitting singles, doubles, and triples regularly.

Take one of the more flashy and "innovative" tools that is out there today, the Healthcare Blue Book. Healthcare Blue Book is a website and app that provides health care pricing transparency information to consumers. In the general version of the platform, the information provided is a range of prices for a particular service within a particular market. The "fair" price for the service is outlined and is intended to give consumers the information they need to shop around to ensure they are getting a good deal on their care. The issue with this is that the pricing information bears little resemblance to the actual pricing a consumer may experience through their insurance plan due to the lack of transparency related to the network discounts their plan receives.

With the more robust version, Healthcare Blue Book or tools like it are integrated into the member portal of a particular insurance carrier, and general pricing information AFTER the network discount is made available. Now we are getting somewhere, but…
Did I mention that I have a Bowflex in my basement? It looks awesome and the guy in the commercial was absolutely ripped. The strange thing is, I haven't gotten in any better shape since I got it. Well no, I haven't used it but I have it and it looks cool! Here's the thing, I've been arguing for transparency in every aspect of the health care supply chain throughout this book. It is an absolute must to achieve a TCHP. That being said, you must do something with the information and tools at your disposal.

As I stated at the outset of the book, employers are ground zero for the revolution. You also must absolutely have your employees onboard as well, but they can't be the frontline as they will fail. There are too many things stacked against any individual as they move through the health care supply chain. Employees on their own are unable to disrupt the status quo.

Let's revisit Healthcare Blue Book to make my point. To get the biggest return on implementing a tool like Healthcare Blue Book, employers are advised to implement financial incentives for employees to use the tool, usually in the form of cash rewards. The idea being, if an employee shops around and saves the plan money, even after sharing some of the savings, the plan comes out ahead. That's great, but once the tool is implemented and up and running, an employer gets to sit back and hope that employees use it, just like my wife hopes I'll actually use the Bowflex. Unfortunately, as we've already covered (all together now) hope is not a strategy. While plan participants may be encouraged to shop around and question their provider as to where they are referring them to go, in reality there are too many obstacles stacked against the end user to expect this to be a truly effective strategy.

Ok, so is there a better way? Well it just so happens there is. You could use strategies like we've already covered, simply contracting with the most cost effective and highest quality providers in your area and excluding all others. That would most definitely ensure the desired results were met. But what if that isn't practical for you, what else could you do?

Case Study: Medical Advocate Program

One of the many innovative vendors working to ensure health plan participants receive care from the highest quality and lowest cost providers is the Medical Advocate Program (MAP). MAP can address multiple needs within a health insurance plan, but for the purposes of this discussion let's focus on their Total Care Program. The foundation of this program is a database of over 6 billion claims, which is updated every 3–6 months. With this data, MAP then engages plan participants to turn the medical plan from a provider-centered plan to a member-centered plan by providing both price and quality information that isn't available from any other source. MAP is able to stratify the provider options by both price and quality to direct plan participants to the best possible provider.

Using this data, MAP is able to proactively steer patients to the best physician to achieve the best possible care at the best possible price. Instead of expecting a plan participant to have the knowledge and information necessary to make the best decision, MAP serves as a concierge for the employees and assures them of an optimal result. There is one key factor that likely goes without saying, but for a tool like MAP to work effectively it can't be voluntary, otherwise it will quickly resemble my Bowflex. This ties back to the role of the employer providing significant messaging surrounding why the plan is built the way it is, and that a TCHP is not the same type of plan that they have become accustomed to. If you keep doing what you've always done…

Every industry is filled with innovators and innovations, and the health care supply chain is no different. While there are many businesses that are truly working to disrupt the status quo and to drive health care costs down, for every one of those there are dozens that are looking to capitalize on the system as it exists today. Why? Because there are billions of dollars flowing through the system, much of which originates with employers.

Case Study: Innovation Institute[31]

The Innovation Institute is a healthcare incubator and leading provider of medical device and healthcare innovation solutions. We are experts in funding and support for healthcare innovation worldwide.

The Innovation Institute is a for-profit, limited liability company owned by non-profit health systems (our equity owners or "Member Owners"). The Innovation Institute is authorized to have seven "Member Owners" as investors. The minimum investment required to be Member Owner is $10 million. This can be a cash investment, or a combination of cash and asset contribution. The Innovation Institute has a unique business model that has allowed it to be profitable from Day One by holding a portfolio of service companies that sell services to hospitals and health systems internationally. The profits from these service companies are reinvested in innovation.

---

[31] https://ii4change.com/, accessed June 2018.

When I came across this organization I initially thought this was a great thing, as these health systems are working together to identify innovations to improve health. Then, as I learned more, I realized this is simply an example of the status quo looking to profit and maintain the status quo. What led me to this conclusion is simply a review of the Innovation Institute's portfolio companies. They include:

- A staffing company
- A company that specializes in people, organization, culture and strategy, and offers integrated solutions to build and sustain human capital capacity and optimize organizational performance
- A HIM coding, auditing, and consulting company founded on uncompromising values and dedicated to the clients it serves, and to each other
- A construction company
- A commercial real-estate brokerage and development company
- A computer networking service provider offering managed networks, structured cabling, and wireless installation services
- An office furniture dealer
- An executive coaching firm
- An engineering firm focused on assisting entities in complying with California's seismic compliance regulations

This example isn't unique in the health care industry either. The largest non-profit health care system in the US, Ascension Health, owns Ascension Holdings which "includes a portfolio of companies that provide innovative services and solutions to healthcare companies in the United States and internationally."[32]

---

[32] https://ascension.org/Our-Work/Ascension-Holdings, accessed June 2018.

This includes a facilities management company, a business transformation services organization, and a group purchasing organization.

If you are paying attention, it is hard for a month to go by without some new innovation being announced. The fact is, the vast majority of them don't address the underlying issues, price, lack of information, and lack of transparency, but rather they are actually new ways to capitalize on the status quo. Whether it is a firm looking to assist with financing the growing health care debt of individuals, or pharmacy benefit managers acquiring health insurance carriers, there are smart individuals carving out their piece of the pie in the current health care supply chain on a daily basis. What if, however, employers sought out and embraced innovations that meaningfully impacted price and transparency with the same eagerness that others in the supply chain are using? It is imperative that employers have a litmus test for the types of innovation they seek out for their plan. They must:

- Affect the price of services
- Increase the information available to plan sponsors
- Improve and enhance transparency at all levels

Employers should be demanding that their advisors consistently present them with new ideas and solutions that pass the litmus test. As members of the NextGen Benefits Mastermind Partnership, my colleagues spend tens of thousands of dollars each year traveling around the country quarterly, to discuss and review the latest innovations that support Total Control Health Plan sponsors. Through this team effort we are able to ensure that we are aware of the latest strategies that pass the innovation litmus test.

Chapter 9
Auto Adjudication

If you've ever been part of a medical administrator RFP process, you've likely come across a question similar to this, "What percentage of your claims are auto adjudicated?" The answers vary, but often the number is upwards of 85% or 90%, which the administrators wear as a badge of honor. I used to think this was good too, as it ensured smooth sailing and little pushback from participants and providers for delayed claim payments. From an administrator's perspective, the more that claims can be auto adjudicated the better as it keeps overhead as low as possible.

Auto-adjudication attempts to find patterns and flag claims for review often based on incomplete or inconsistent data. Even the best, most updated auto-adjudication setup is going to miss things. In high-cost claims for complicated health situations like inpatient stays, auto-adjudication assumes that all costs are (A.) Necessary, and (B.) Truthful, but that is not always the case. For example: No patient is ever immediately discharged from the ICU; their level of care is appropriately downgraded to less intensive and less costly levels as their health improves. Yet consistently claims are filed that do not accommodate this level of care, requesting reimbursement for an ICU stay until the moment of discharge, and many auto-adjudication programs miss this. Billing codes and diagnosis codes match, and preauthorization may have been obtained, so the claim passes auto-adjudication, even though it is unlikely to have occurred as billed.[33]

---

[33] https://www.mdstrat.com/the-true-cost-of-auto-adjudication/ accessed June 2018.

Here is the issue with this. The vast majority of medical claims are submitted on the UB04 form developed by the Centers for Medicare and Medicaid Services to streamline the claims paying process. The UB04 form contains all of the relevant pieces of information a computer needs to process claims, however there is very little detail contained on the form that outlines exactly what occurred.

For example, a UBO4 form may list that 10 units of saline solution were ordered prior to a particular surgical procedure, which the computer approves as it falls within the guidelines for that procedure. However, upon reviewing the detailed case notes, it becomes clear that only 2 units were actually needed and administered in this case. How many units do you believe your plan should pay for, the 2 that were used or all 10 that were ordered? If it were my plan, I'd only pay for the 2 units used, but with a plan being auto adjudicated I wouldn't have the information necessary or the opportunity to make that call. Of course, I wouldn't actually be making that decision but I'd want the plan administrator that I'd hired to be doing exactly that.

According to a 2016 NBC News Story, *"Accounts of medical billing errors vary widely. While the American Medical Association estimated that 7.1 percent of paid claims in 2013 contained an error, a 2014 NerdWallet study found mistakes in 49 percent of Medicare claims. Groups that review bills on patients' behalf, including Medical Billing Advocates of America and CoPatient, put the error rate closer to 75 or 80 percent."*[34]

Regardless of the percentage, from a payer standpoint one error is too many and I'd want to be sure that I am only paying the correct charges. For this reason, there is a growing number of independent third party administrators moving away from auto adjudication and

---

[34] https://www.nbcnews.com/business/consumer/it-s-time-get-second-opinion-paying-medical-bill-n545626, accessed June 2018.

shifting back to manual claims processing. Some administrators auto adjudicate less than 20 percent of the claims they receive, allowing for an individual to review the claims to increase the likelihood of catching billing errors or ineligible charges.

As you might suspect at this point, there are businesses that have capitalized on the lack of transparency within the health care supply chain at every level, and auto adjudication offers another opportunity for more waste. Take, for example, the industry of outsourced billing services for physician practices. There are many players within this space who promise many advantages over handling the billing in-house, including efficiency, lower payroll costs, reduced training costs, fewer errors, and most important higher revenue. Higher revenue, how can that be if they are billing for the same things? What these firms have learned is how to tweak the way in which the bill is submitted, for example, by unbundling services while still making it through the auto adjudication system to drive higher revenue. Take for example, this quote from one vendor's website, *"A company that focuses on medical billing, and not medical care delivery, usually has state-of-the-art technology and a staff trained to maximize coding for higher revenue capture. More money in, and less money out."*[35]

An interesting exercise would be to request to review some claims as they are submitted to your current administrator to see the level of detail that commonly accompanies each claim. Then request to see all of the case notes associated with the claim to see how much additional information is actually associated with certain claims. Can't get the information? You are not in control.

From the perspective of a health insurance administrator, especially a fully-insured carrier constrained by the limits of the Minimum Loss Ratio discussed previously, it makes complete

---

[35] https://www.adsc.com/blog/7-ways-outsourcing-your-medical-billing-will-benefit-your-practice, accessed June 2018.

sense to maximize efficiencies wherever possible. Industry specifics peg the cost of manually adjudicating a claim at $4 per claim, where an auto adjudicated claim costs only $1. Additionally, while all administrators have no intention of processing invalid claims, at the end of the day, it doesn't really impact the plans if they do. Whether it is the incentive to see claims increase due to the MLR or the fact that increased costs are simply baked into future premium, the liability falls to employers. From a self-insured standpoint, the claims dollars simply flow through to the employer.

With a TCHP however, an employer may elect to pay a high administrative fee for a greater number of claims to be manually adjudicated. A review of past claims would likely identify for a particular employer where the sweet spot is, and a TCHP would allow them to capitalize on this opportunity.

Case Study: Cypress Benefit Administrators

Cypress Benefit Administrators is an independent TPA based out of Appleton, Wisconsin. Their auto adjudication rate is closer to 20%, and they have also invested heavily in technology that helps them to identify the pocket change (flakes of gold) that often easily flow through plans. I've never panned for gold, but I've seen it on TV enough to know that all of those little flakes can add up to a bar of gold pretty quickly. The following is a case study outlining the success they've had helping clients pan for gold.

Cypress Benefit Administrators has worked to develop the most all-encompassing fraud protection and cost containment system available: ARGUS Claim Review. Here is one example of how many of Cypress clients have experienced significant savings generated by ARGUS:

A heart institute billed the following CPT codes: 33960 - Prolonged extracorporeal circulation for cardiopulmonary insufficiency, initial 24 hours; and 33961 - Prolonged extracorporeal circulation for cardiopulmonary insufficiency, each additional 24 hours. These codes were listed separately in addition to a code for a primary procedure on the same date of service. Obviously, there can't be 48 houses worth of treatment in one day. CPT 33961 was denied and was not questioned by the provider. Total savings to the client, $1,357.00.

There are also multiple bars of gold that can be found with a little extra mining with larger claims.

As a matter of policy, Veteran's Administration Hospitals do not negotiate with private insurance companies or Third Party Administrators. They also do not participate in any PPO or HMO networks. Therefore, their charges are always considered out of network, exposing the plan to greater financial risk. The Veteran's Administration Hospitals are supposed to bill "reasonable" charges, although at times ARGUS Claim Review has found that charges from these hospitals can be a bit more than reasonable.

Cypress received a bill from a Veterans Administration Hospital for a four-day inpatient stay in the about of $101,575.28. When reviewing large claims and beginning the negotiations process, ARGUS built a case by collecting and preparing hard data to substantiate the amount that was offered to pay on behalf of the clients.

Since the VA Hospitals charges are not eligible for Medicare reimbursement, they do not have a Medicare Provider Identification Number that normally allows ARGUS to compare their charges to what Medicare would pay the same hospital for that bill. However, ARGUS has the capability to look up the Medicare national pay rate for the Diagnosis Related Group

(DRG) before it is adjusted for several factors, including the local wage index, number of days inpatient, outlier costs, etc.

Based on the DRG submitted, the Medicare national pay rate for the inpatient stay was $6,280.30. As part of the data gathering and preparation process, ARGUS also located two hospitals within a 50 mile radius of the VA Hospital and ran the claim data to see what Medicare would pay those two hospitals if the same bill was submitted o them. The amounts were that Medicare would pay $10,020.03 and $11,46.71 respectively.

While trying to negotiate a fair compensation for services, ARGUS Claim Review, used the higher of the two rates, $11,456.71, and paid the VA Hospital 200% of that amount: $22,913.42.

The total savings for the inpatient stay came to an astounding $78,664.86.

Chapter 10
Brokers Haven't Influenced Price

According to the 2016 Society for Human Resources Management (SHRM) Strategic Benefits: Health Care survey, 66% of employers are very concerned about controlling health care costs, while 31% are somewhat concerned. These results are not surprising in any way, as health care costs have risen consistently year over year for the last 20+ years, taking up a larger and larger percentage of employer budgets. According to the same survey, 73% of respondents reported an increase in costs for 2016.

We've been over this already, costs are going up. I bring this up again to make a different point. Employers can't be experts at everything, they need to focus on what they are very good at and then hire good help for the things they're not. For example, rarely do you see an employer representing themselves in court, or filing their own taxes, or assembling their own office furniture. The same is true with health insurance. While there is nothing standing in the way of an employer going directly to an insurance carrier to buy a policy, the vast majority of employers work with an insurance agent. The number one reason employers do so is to help them address cost. But why then, if there are hundreds of thousands of insurance agents around the country whose primary job it is to help employers address cost, do costs keep going up?

From my perspective, employers have been saying one thing and doing another. While they say that cost is important to them, the message they have been sending to the agent community is that any number of other things, besides cost, are the priority. As I will outline in this chapter, employers need to rethink what is really important to them from an insurance agent, and change the way they communicate that to the market if they expect to achieve a different result.

The first thing that needs to be discussed is that first and foremost insurance agents are salespeople. Internally, insurance agents are often referred to as "producers" because it is their job to produce for the agency. Generally speaking, if they don't sell you something they don't get paid. While agents may use different terms like broker, advisor, consultant, or counselor, at the end of the day insurance agents are salespeople and it is their job to convince you to buy from them. This isn't necessarily a bad thing, but you need to keep this mind as we review the next key points.

The barriers to entry into the insurance business, especially employee benefits, are very low from an education and infrastructure standpoint. If you want to become an employee benefits insurance agent, you could likely do so within a month and it would only take that long due to the limited schedule for the mandatory pre-licensing class. Once you had your license, you could start getting appointed with carriers and you'd be off to the races. Finally, with few exceptions, all agents have access to the same stuff at the same price. Heck, in many states there is software that quotes every available plan for you.

Ok, so let's piece this all together:
- Insurance agents are sales people
- Just about anyone can become an insurance agent
- They all have access to the same stuff at the same price

Let's equate this reality to buying a car. If you want to buy a Chevy, you will likely shop around from Chevy dealer to Chevy dealer, looking for the best price. While they may offer you other bells and whistles like free oil changes or a free loaner car, the number one thing motivating you is the price the dealer will offer you. Now, what if every dealer sold identical cars at the same price? The dynamic would shift and you would start paying far more attention to the bells and whistles. Who was closest, had the nicest waiting room, would pick you up and drop you off when you needed service. This is the world that most insurance agents/agencies live in today.

As employers shop for agents/brokers, they are showered with a laundry list of bells and whistles that have no meaningful impact on the cost of insurance. These include:
- Compliance assistance
- Benefit web portals
- Customized communication materials
- Smartphone apps
- Being an extension of the HR department
- Claims assistance
- Handling administrative duties

While all of these are nice and some are important: is an insurance agency the best place to get them? Let me put it this way, what if your law firm lost every case they represented for you and provided bad advice, but they also offered you all the free legal pads you could use and a website to store all of your legal documents? Chances are, you'd look for different representation and you'd buy your legal pads from Staples.

Why then does this sort of thing happen every day in the insurance agency world? The number one reason, in my opinion, that this has happed is that employee benefits and therefore health insurance, have been directed to the HR department for management. This is in no way a slam on the HR department, but rather a statement that the things that are important to the typical HR department are unrelated to a P&L statement. Take, for example, this answer I recently received from a friend who is a controller at an 800-employee firm when I asked who handles their insurance, "for P&C, I would recommend our finance director, and for benefits our HR VP." Why is it that something that is typically the second or third line on a P&L is directed to HR, and something far lower down the list is directed to finance? .

The clear answer is that employee benefits and therefore health insurance, are directly tied to employees which falls under the leadership of HR. That is logical and makes sense, but the risk this raises is that finance and HR look at the world through completely different lenses and frankly they have different priorities. This isn't the case with every employer as often a CEO or CFO would attend renewal meetings, but when the question was asked, "Who handles your employee benefits?" The answer is almost always HR. As a result, having health insurance under the view of HR has shifted the focus from financial controls to other priorities such as customer service and compliance.

For the CEOs, Presidents, and CFOs reading this book, let me let you in on a little secret. Generally speaking, HR departments HATE insurance. Additionally, I've yet to come across a HR department with too big a budget and too many people on staff. The exact opposite is true. The average HR department has a very small budget. Rarely do they have enough people to get everything done, and guess what, they deal with people all day everyday. No matter how organized they are, since people are the primary focus there isn't a messier department around. One of my favorite things to do when spending time with a HR person is to ask them about the craziest thing they've had to deal with in their career. The answer is never related to the time the payroll system went haywire or the time the time clocks didn't work. No, they are always about some crazy people-related story and boy are they good. If you haven't done this recently, carve out a few minutes in your schedule and go talk to the first HR person you can find. You're in for a treat.

Here is the other thing, not only do HR departments hate insurance, but they hate insurance companies too, and frankly many don't have much of a desire to spend a lot of time with the people that sell it either. If you want to have a little fun some time, sign up to go to a HR event, and when you get there, sit at a table full of people you don't know. Then as you go around the table and make your introductions, say this "Hi my name is (fill in your name) and I'm in HR at (say your company)." Then wait a few seconds as everyone nods and smiles, then say this. "Actually I'm kidding, I'm an employee benefits agent." The blood will drain out of their faces faster than a barometer drops in a hurricane. Why is this? Because insurance agents are salespeople. Sure, they can be charming and funny (I like to think that I am) and take you golfing, but insurance agents are in sales and HR people hear from 4,500 of them every year 3 months before your insurance renews. Additionally, what if you went to work every day intent on addressing areas of strategic importance to your company, like succession planning or increasing employee retention, but without fail most days you found yourself spending time on hold with an insurance company trying to resolve another claim issue for one of your frustrated employees? You'd be pretty happy about it, right? Or not.

So for the non-HR people reading this book, put yourself in their shoes. If you were regularly being told that all insurance agents get the same price, and in fact that many of them won't even quote insurance without first becoming the agent of record, what factors would you use to choose an agent? Well, if it were me, I'd be inclined to go with the one who told me that they'd take all of the administrative headaches off of my plate like adding and removing employees from the plan and dealing with claim issues. If they'd handle compliance for me and offer me a HR technology platform as well, even better. How about the cost of insurance though, what about that? Well, everyone has been saying that it is driven by trend and we've been coming in below that, so we're good.

So this is where we find ourselves today. As insurance has become more and more commoditized and competition has increased among agencies, the agent/broker community has looked to differentiate themselves in a crowded market. With HR being the primary buyer of employee benefits, they have tailored their message to the wants and needs of the HR department. The result is that agents/brokers have not worked to differentiate themselves by providing solutions to the reality of increasing costs, but rather by providing more value added services than the other guy. I would argue that this is a tacit admission that an agency is unable to address the cost of insurance, the primary reason they are hired, in a meaningful way.

What I mean by this is that in order to compete with the other agencies in their market, an agency needs to be able to check certain boxes. For example, to be taken seriously today an agency needs to have an online platform to assist employers with online enrollment and benefit communication. While potentially attractive during the sales process, chances are that in most cases each agency only has one solution and therefore they work to force that solution into every setting. The reality is, however, that given an objective review of the actual needs of a particular employer there is a high likelihood that an alternative solution would be a better fit. To add to this, in many cases agencies charge their clients for access to these systems.

The end result of this arrangement is that an employer gets tied to a particular agency due to the "sticky" nature of the value added service that a firm provides, while nothing meaningful is done to address costs. Insurance agents and agencies have done a good job of convincing employers that this is how they should be judged and the circle goes around and around. Take for example, a RFP for *employee benefits insurance broker and consulting services* I found online with a simple Google search. I've responded to dozens of these over the years and they are all largely the same. Here are some sample questions that the competing agencies are being asked to respond to:

- What is your approach when shopping for bids or negotiating renewals, and how would you differentiate XYZ Company to insurers? How would XYZ Company benefit from your market position?
- Briefly describe the firm's system of quality control to ensure the work meets a high quality standard.
- Briefly describe how familiar you are with products and carriers for all lines of coverage including health, stop loss/reinsurance, wellness, dental, vision, life, disability, long-term care and voluntary benefits and how you determine which carrier's products to review for renewal purposes.
- Describe whether you have experience with clients that are similar to XYZ Company's industry and employer type (e.g., education, non-ERISA, joint powers agency).

Scope of Services and Proposed Project Schedule

Briefly describe the firm's understanding of the scope of services to be provided, including but not limited to:

- What your role is in the management of the benefit plans including evaluating health related risks, offering suggestions on how to reduce the company's claims experience and premiums, and assisting with escalated claims resolution/issues?
- Include whether your firm employs an in-house actuary for providing detailed analysis of claims data, stop loss risk, workforce demographic analysis, funding options, trends, premium ratios, reserves, IBNR reporting and actuarial

value of plan design changes. If yes, please provide credentials.
- Does your firm assist with recommendations for setting employee contributions? Do you provide benefit rate sheets with COBRA rate equivalents and imputed income calculations? If so, please provide a sample.
- Describe how your firm stays current with state regulations that impact multi-state employers and what resources you provide to your clients to stay compliant.
- Include whether your firm employs an in-house benefits/compliance attorney. If so, please provide his/her credentials and examples of communications provided to clients. If not, do you use an external benefits/compliance attorney and if so, which firm do you use?
- What resources do you provide to help manage benefits and outline a benefits strategy? Please provide a sample of the materials and reports that you use as a part of your regular reviews.
- What tools do you use to stay on top of any ongoing or outstanding action items?
- What benchmarking surveys do you use/provide to determine whether XYZ Company's benefits/renewal proposals are competitive with similar organizations?
- Describe the technology tools you use and any you make available to your clients and if there are plans in place to enhance your current technology/tools.
- What role does your firm play in facilitating Open Enrollment? Please provide examples of any communications.
- Does your firm provide any value added benefits (e.g., wellness program, benefits enrollment systems, health care advocacy)? If so, are there additional fees for these services?

- Identify which Account Managers from Aetna and Kaiser would most likely be assigned to work with XYZ Company through your firm.

The reason I list all of these questions is to make the point that I believe employers have been looking in the wrong place. With regards to this RFP, keep in mind that trained salespeople are responding to it, and as a result they know exactly what answer to plug into every one of these questions. To add to this, the answers are likely canned. Take, for example, the fact that the Society for Human Resources Management recently launched a new broker finder tool where employers can search for just the right insurance agent. The tool is marketed to insurance agents too, and for $750 a year I can build a database of "reusable responses to employer questions." Put another way, I can build a library of canned answers to use each time an employer sends me a questionnaire like the one above.

It's not that the answers to some of these questions aren't important, but the vast majority of them are unrelated to the ultimate job at hand—reducing the cost of health insurance. I believe there is a better way to identify the right advisor partner, which I will review shortly, but here is what I feel is wrong with the current RFP model. I have yet to meet an employer that actually enjoys this process. I've met many HR people and other business leaders who stay with an existing agency they are unhappy with simply because they don't want to go through this process, and I don't blame them. Completing a RFP is a mind-numbing, soul crushing experience and I can't imagine reading the answers to more than one of them, especially when most of the answers are exactly the same.

So what is an employer to do? How do they go about finding the right advisor for them? The first step is to divide all of the services

you get from your agent/agency today into two buckets. They should be:
1. Solutions to address cost
2. Everything else, such as:
   a. Administrative services
   b. Technology
   c. Employee engagement
   d. Wellness
   e. Compliance
   f. Claim issues

Then determine what you are willing to pay for those services. Here is a little secret, employee benefit agents are paid very well, often based on commissions on the various products they sell you. I am not stating this because it is a mystery, but you need to understand what may be influencing the recommendations you are getting. If you are getting good and effective advice, it may be worth every penny. But, here's the deal. Agencies often add all of the value added services to justify their compensation but in reality the bells and whistles they are providing aren't that expensive. Let's take a look at some to make the point.

Compliance: This often falls into two buckets, 5500 filing if it is required for you, and compliance documents. There is absolute value in this because employers are required to do it, so if you aren't getting it from an agency you'll either need to do it yourself or find someone else to do it. Here's the secret though, filing a 5500 shouldn't cost more that $500 to $600. From a compliance document(s) standpoint, it shouldn't cost more than $750 to $1,250.

HR Technology: This is a big one for me. I absolutely believe in working smarter not harder, and in 2018 every employer should have a solid HR technology platform to increase efficiency, reduce errors, and reduce administrative burdens. The reality is, however,

that many employers don't have anything or are nursing along antiquated technology. Why is this? My experience tells me that there are two reasons:
1. Those who control the purse strings don't see the need or value in investing in such a system.
2. The time and expense of upgrading to a new system.

I don't believe either of these reasons are valid and here is why. HR in general, and employee benefits specifically, are very transactional and have historically involved a lot of paper. This is incredibly inefficient and in 2018 it simply doesn't have to be. If I were the HR person working for a business that wouldn't (I use that word intentionally) afford an effective HR system, I'd be all over the fact that I could get one from an insurance agency and this is why they offer them. Typically, agencies select one solution and then either offer it for free to clients or pass it along for a fee. Now for a peek behind the curtain, the systems are not that expensive (one of the most popular systems in the market today costs agencies about $10,000 to $12,000 per year, total for unlimited clients), and often they don't do everything an HR department is actually looking for. But, if you take advantage of the system made available to you and start building processes around it, now you are stuck. Disregard that the insurance advice isn't driving profit to your bottom line, you can't function without the HR system and so you aren't going anywhere.

I have spent a lot of time over my career researching different technology platforms and I have yet to find the perfect system. The closest I have come is what I have seen from some of the companies disrupting the payroll market such as Paycor and Paylocity, and this makes sense. Why, you ask? If you think about the fact everything HR does revolves around the employee, and the reason an employee comes to work is to get paid, then using a payroll system as the hub for your HR system makes sense. What companies like Paycor have done is build an endlessly scalable web-based platform that seamlessly provides solutions to most HR challenges, and it is worth noting that the entrenched incumbents are lagging way behind from an innovation standpoint. From applicant tracking and onboarding at the front end, to employee reviews and termination on the back end, these systems have the ability to do it all. In addition, they are constantly getting better based on customer feedback and they are positioned to evolve with their customers. The best part is, as with many things in technology, they keep getting better while the costs remain highly competitive.

So what is my point? My point is that HR technology is incredibly important, but for the reasons stated above and others, your employee benefits agent may not be the best source. This certainly won't be true in every case, but you should know if it is true for you and not let the lure of a free shiny object take your eye off the primary goal of reducing the cost of your health insurance.

Administration: This is an easy one. If you have the right technology solution, administration should not be a complicated or time consuming task. Insurance agencies that want to grow know this too. It is not sustainable for them to simply employ people to take administrative tasks off the plate of their client. As a result, many are forcing clients to use a technology platform to simplify administration. If they are doing this to increase their efficiency, so can you. Agencies invest in technology to track each "transaction" they handle for clients, one for accuracy, but equally so that they can provide stewardship reports to clients to show them how much they are doing for them. If that is what are you are looking for in an agent, great, but how much are you willing to pay for that service and is it more valuable than seeing your health insurance costs go down?

Claims: I've been looking for the last 17 years, but I have yet to see a bumper sticker that says, "Have you hugged your health insurance company today?" People love to hate insurance companies—largely because they are easy to hate. In their defense, I'd say some of it is justified and some of it isn't. As covered earlier in the chapter on management, individuals need to change their perspective in terms of what they expect from an insurance company. If they want something that covers everything, anywhere, all the time, they need to be prepared to pay for it. If they aren't willing to pay for it, then they need to be prepared to be more flexible. That being said, no one likes sitting on hold and experiencing poor customer service. Frankly, customer service is a huge source of frustration for insurance agents too, because they are selling someone else's stuff and have little to no control over the customer experience.

The good news is there is a solution, the Total Control Health Plan. Let me explain.

As covered throughout this book, a TCHP is unique to each employer and it is the product of bringing multiple service providers together to achieve the best result. Many of the service providers operate with a "have it your way" mindset, dramatically reducing the "thank you sir, may I have another" situations common to prepackage solutions. Additionally, those managing a TCHP are seeking out small, entrepreneurial businesses who are looking to disrupt the status quo. What this means is that if the owner/president/CEO isn't answering the phone, you can very likely get them on the phone if absolutely necessary. I hate sitting on hold and with a TCHP it doesn't have to be that way.

The role of the insurance agent, consultant, broker, has changed. The brokering aspect of the business can and is being done by computers and rarely do agents negotiate significantly better deals than everyone else competing for your business. What employers need today is a health plan construction manager. Think about it this way, if you were going to build a new building or add an addition, your first step would likely be hiring a construction manager. They would then serve as your representative, working with every player in the supply chain from architects to subcontractors to the building inspector to ensure that the project comes in on time, and on budget. They speak the language and know who is the best fit for each component of the project. Next generation benefit advisors understand their role as the construction manager, helping their clients to build the best health insurance plan that meets their needs and fits their budget.

Now that you have outlined the services you expect to receive from your insurance agent and what you are wiling to pay for them, go out and find the right partner for you. My suspicion is that you are going to find a lot of agents/agencies that look very similar to one another, and very few that have built their business around cost reduction. Since you are reading this book, I am going to assume the cost of your health insurance plan is very important to you. If that is true, then be sure to design your compensation model to reinforce the items that are important to you. If an agent/agency is serious about reducing your costs, then they should absolutely be willing to tie their compensation to their ability to do so. The advisors within my peer group all have and do base their compensation on their performance. There is significant value in the expertise they bring to the table and the work that they do to establish and manage a TCHP, and they should be paid fairly for that. However, some of their compensation should be tied to their ability to achieve the desired results, so there is perfect alignment between their objectives and the employers.

It is also important to note that bigger is often equated with better, and the same is often true when employers select advisers. For example, think back to the RFP questions listed earlier in this chapter and the question about having an in-house actuary. If a firm answered "no" to that question, it would likely be seen as a negative. The fact is that having an in-house actuary, or legal team, or compliance team, shouldn't influence an employer's decision to hire a firm so long as they can address those needs by leveraging outside partners. In my experience, smaller, boutique firms have proven to be the primary drivers of innovation for a number of reasons, including:

- They have to be more innovative to compete against big regional and national players.
- They have the ability to be nimble.
- They are not tied to corporate initiatives or strategic partnerships that may influence the recommendations made.
- You are often dealing with an owner or partner, which inherently brings a higher level of accountability.

Finally, when your TCHP performs as expected, you will find yourself with financial resources you hadn't previously had which you can then invest into whatever you choose, like outside compliance assistance, or HR technology, etc.

Chapter 11
What I Haven't Talked About...Yet

As you are nearing the end of this book, you may have noticed that there were a number of items that have likely been part of discussions you have had in the past related to insurance that I haven't touched on. It wasn't an oversight, but rather intentional. From my perspective, they shouldn't influence the decision to implement a TCHP. To illustrate the point, here are a few examples.

Plan Design

One of the biggest items that I haven't spent any time on is plan design, because frankly it doesn't matter. Playing with plan design, without addressing the underlying causes of cost increases is simply rearranging the deck chairs on the Titanic. The ship is going down. Rather than moving chairs around, I'd prefer to look for a new ship. Speaking frankly, if the advisors you are currently working with, or are considering working with, talk to you about plan design then they don't get it. Whether it is the new industry flavor of the week like Value Based Insurance Design or something else, talking about plan design is wasted effort.

In *The Company That Solved Health Care*, John Torinus, Jr. attributes much of their success in reducing costs to the implementation of consumer-driven plans with high deductibles. For comparison, in 2004 when they implemented the high deductible health plans (HDHP), the deductibles they implemented were $750, $1,000, and $1,500, compared to the average deductible in 2003 for a PPO of $275, for a single person. Here are a few things to consider about what the market has done since that time.

- HSAs were created in 2003 and the minimum deductible of $1,000 and elimination of co-pays were a big departure from the plans employees knew. Today, high deductibles are the norm, and costs continue to rise year over year.
- There is a law of diminishing returns as deductibles are raised. The number of plan participants who incur claims between $250 and $1,000 is greater than the number who incur claims between $1,000 and $2,000. Logically, by making the jump from $250 to $750 or higher, employers such as Serigraph saw a significant reduction in claim exposure to the plan due to the additional liability now absorbed by the member.
- Initially, the expectation was that consumer driven plans would drive participants to approach buying health care as they do everything else, by shopping around. Rather than simply foregoing treatments, plan participants would seek the most cost effective provider to have the procedure done. While true to a small degree, the data has shown that generally speaking participants have simply elected to forego treatment, which is not a positive outcome.

Take this brief summary of the results of a 2015 study on the impacts of a transition to a HDHP/HSA plan at one very large employer from an article in VOX:

Economists Zarek Brot-Goldberg, Amitabh Chandra, Benjamin Handel, and Jonathan Kolstad studied *a firm that, in 2013, shifted tens of thousands of workers into high-deductible insurance plans. This was a perfect moment to look at how their patterns of care changed—whether they did, in fact, use the new shopping tools their employer gave them to compare prices.*

Turns out they didn't. The new paper shows that when faced with a higher deductible, patients did not price shop for a better deal. Instead, both healthy and sick patients simply used way less health care.

"I am a little bit surprised at just how poorly patients were able to do when looking at very similar products, like MRI scans, and with a shopping tool," says Kolstad, an economist at University of California Berkeley and one of the study's co-authors. "Two years in, and there's still no evidence they're price shopping."[36]

- Most insurers priced HDHPs very favorably for the first 3–5 years of their existence, however many of them discovered over time that they had underpriced them and eventually sizable rate increases were passed along.

Think about it this way, changing plan design is simply determining how much risk you are going to shift to the end user to reduce how much premium an employer pays or in the case of a self-insured plan, how much of each claim the plan pays. Does raising a co-pay or a deductible do anything to effect the price of the services? Sure, some may argue that consumer driven plans like Health Savings Accounts are intended to get the user to shop around. I've had a HSA for over a decade and the last time I checked the premiums haven't gone down yet. As covered earlier in the book, for an HSA plan to work, every single user on the plan must aggressively negotiate the best possible deal for each service in a system with absolutely no transparency. It hasn't and won't happen, which is why an employer needs to take charge at the plan level.

My colleagues throughout the country in the NextGen Benefits Mastermind Partnership approach plan design in a different way. It

---

[36] https://www.vox.com/2015/10/14/9528441/high-deductible-insurance-kolstad, accessed June 2018.

is the last item on the list when working with clients once the Total Control Health Plan infrastructure is in place, and the discussion is often surrounding how we make the plan better. Imagine presenting a plan with no deductibles and no copays if the member takes certain steps as Walmart has done. That's a discussion about plan design I'd like to have.

Fixed Costs

For those of you reading the book who currently have a self-insured plan or are familiar with how they work, you may have noticed I haven't covered fixed costs associated with a TCHP. These costs include things like administration, stop-loss, medical management, etc. The reason I haven't covered these is that the fixed costs associated with a TCHP may be much different than what you've experienced before. From an administrative cost standpoint, commonly independent TPAs are far less expensive than a commercial carrier. That being said, as you dive into the "why" behind how your plan is performing, it will likely become clear that there are areas that need additional help. If you are working with a results-oriented advisor, he/she will present you with a number of innovative, entrepreneurial solutions to the challenges your plan faces. Ultimately, you may elect to spend more on fixed costs than you do today because you are confident that the partners you've selected will deliver far greater savings. If done correctly, the additional fixed costs will be tied to performance guarantees in order to ensure the appropriate ROI is realized.

From a stop-loss perspective, a sponsor of a TCHP should expect to see reductions in their stop-loss costs, and in some cases significant reductions. For example, one RBP administrator has established relationships with stop-loss providers who offer a 30% reduction in premium if the RBP model is implemented. This makes sense, as a plan sponsor works to manage their health care supply chain as they do every other aspect of their business, the exposure the plan has will go down. Ultimately it is this exposure that a stop-loss carrier is insuring and therefore a reduction in exposure will result in a reduction in premium. Pretty cool, huh?

Coalitions

While almost any employer with 50 or more employees can implement their own TCHP, it is true there is strength in numbers. Groups like Amazon, Berkshire Hathaway, JP Morgan, and Walmart can dramatically move the needle on a national scale due to the size of their populations. For smaller employers however, the only needle that matters is theirs. That being said, for years my colleagues in the NextGen Benefits Mastermind Partnership have been helping smaller employers join together to form coalitions so that they can exert greater leverage as larger employers do. Industry thought leaders, Bob Gearhart Sr. and Bob Gearhart Jr., owners of DCW Group in Ohio, have had great success with their Valley Health Coalition by leveraging the buying power of like-minded small- and medium-sized businesses in their area. 2017 Employee Benefit Advisor of the year, Mick Rogers of Axial Benefits in Massachusetts, has been using this approach since 2009, saving coalition partners millions of dollars in the process. The formation of coalitions, whether industry specific or not, is a very logical approach that should be considered as employers look to continually refine their Total Control Health Plan. However, coalitions are only successful if the members within them are all pulling in the same direction. Therefore, it can be viewed like this: Not every sponsor of a TCHP needs to be in a coalition, but every member of a coalition needs to have a TCHP.

Onsite Clinics

Forward-thinking employers have been utilizing onsite or near site clinics to increase access to providers and reduce costs for decades.

I am a big believer in onsite clinics when implemented correctly and I believe when practical an employer should seriously consider implementing one. The operative word there, however, is practical. There are many reasons ranging from cost to geography that make onsite or even near site clinics impractical for a majority of employers. Additionally, while a clinic would certainly complement an employer's TCHP, they aren't a necessity to have one. To use an analogy, if a TCHP was a car engine, an onsite clinic would be nitrous oxide.

Value-Based Payments

Following the implementation of the Affordable Care Act, the concept of value-based payments have gotten a lot more attention. While taking many different forms, the concept behind value based payments is departing from the purely volume based model most payers use today to a model that rewards efficiency and quality. As sponsors of TCHP work to establish transparent and efficient relationships with providers, this is certainly one approach that may be considered. That being said, in a transparent relationship where both parties are on a level footing, there may be other payment models that are equally effective. Therefore, value based payments may have a role within your TCHP, however it is possible to achieve the same results with different models as well.

E-Visits

Leveraging technology to drive quality, efficiency, and to deliver a better user experience is a cornerstone of Total Control Health Plans. From my perspective, tele-health and virtual visits have gone mainstream at this point and their inclusion in a TCHP goes without saying.

Chapter 12
Complacency

One of the often overlooked impacts of the Affordable Care Act was the elimination of annual and lifetime limits. Prior to the passage of the ACA, it was common for plans to put caps on the amount of covered benefits in the form of annual or lifetime limits, or both. After a three-year phase-in, no annual limits on covered benefits were allowed by 2014, and initially there was relatively little impact to plans as a result. However, when reviewing the frequency of claims in excess of $1 million prior to the elimination of annual limits and subsequently, stop-loss carriers have seen increases ranging from 350% to over 1,000% over a five-year period. These have been driven both by medical claims and specialty pharmacy claims as the administrative hassles of seeking alternative payment sources for patients who ran up against their annual limits were eliminated.

Where there were incentives in the past to stay under the annual caps, there no longer are and miraculously the once rare idea of claims exceeding $1 million annually are now quite common. The point is, that it is a jungle out there. Effective and savvy business leaders are leveraging the current system to their advantage to build highly profitable businesses, while no one is effectively advocating for the payers and end users.
As I touched on at the beginning of the book, both employers and employees are in a tough spot. For employers, what was once the crown jewel of an employee benefit package is quickly losing its luster and starting to resemble an anchor. For employees, their increasing payroll deductions are eating away at their income while they are also now responsible for a much greater share of

expenses as claims are incurred. With the average deductible for employer-sponsored coverage increasing from $275 in 2003 to $1,505 in 2017, according to the Kaiser Family Foundation, individuals now represent a greater source of payment to providers than ever before. A 2015 Harvard study found that 62% of personal bankruptcies were due to medical expenses and of those filing for bankruptcy, 72% of them had health insurance. Employers and their health insurance plans are inextricably linked and if employers aren't able to control the cost of their plans, it will become a significant liability.

The direction health insurance is headed is undeniable and there is almost universal agreement that it is unsustainable. This is why it is so perplexing why so many employers elect to stay the course. Year over year I hear business owners compare their health insurance rates to their own products and services, and they opine on how they wish they could increase their own prices in the same way insurance costs go up each year. But, they can't. Why? Because they operate in a functional market where their customers and competition wouldn't allow it.

I understand that change is hard and few, if any, employers started their business so that they could run a health insurance plan. Complacency and acceptance of the status quo is eating away at employer profits and it doesn't have to be that way. My NextGen Benefits Mastermind Partnership colleague, Gary Becker of Becker Benefit Group in Maryland, recently shared a cartoon illustrating a long line of people following an arrow labeled "simple but wrong" over a cliff, while only a few followed the "complex but right" arrow, which felt very applicable to this discussion.

The status quo certainly is the path of least resistance, but it only takes a quick review of what the status quo cost 10 years ago compared to today to realize that things must change. Employers must use the same management techniques and strategies that have made their businesses successful on their health insurance plan. It can and is being done, and employers who have figured it out are at a significant competitive advantage.

Employers should not accept proposals that don't address the price of health care services, and without a doubt shouldn't accept a compensation structure for their advisor that isn't tied to performance. Additionally, business leaders must identify their priorities related to their health insurance plan, and if cost is the driving factor they should strongly consider taking management of the health insurance plan off the plate of the HR department. Just because it is the way it has always been done, doesn't mean it should continue that way. Most HR department heads will thank you for giving them more time to focus on strategic HR priorities, and with the finance team focusing on the financial side of the plan, results will follow. It will absolutely require a change of mindset throughout the entire leadership team as change is hard and employees have been conditioned to complain to HR when they don't get the result they want. A TCHP will be different, it isn't the blank credit card that employees have grown accustomed to, but with time and effort it will be far superior.

Undoubtedly, some reading this book will completely disagree with me for reasons varying from simply having a vested interest in the status quo, to challenging the solutions I present which is completely fine. Ultimately, it is up to each business leader to reach their own conclusion, but here are some things to consider as you determine what is the next best step for your business.

- Do you agree that health insurance is expensive because health care is expensive?
- Do you currently have the ability to influence the price of health care in any meaningful way?

- Modeling out your average increase to your plan over the last 3 or 5 or 10 years, at what point will the trend become unsustainable for you?
- How does it compare to your annual price increases for your company's products or services?
- What will you do when you get to the point it is unsustainable?
- Will your employees have revolted before then?

If, after reviewing the questions above, you've come to the conclusion that something needs to change, then a Total Control Health Plan might be for you. Certainly there are many different directions that you could go, but that's the point. Whether you elect to build your own TCHP or drop insurance in lieu of a fine, or any number of other strategies, the time has come for a change. Employers have been blindfolded and playing poker with all of the other players in the health care supply chain for too long. They must remove the blindfold so that they can play on a level playing field and have a fighting chance. At this stage, enough employers have reached this conclusion that those who follow won't be the early adopters.

Change is coming at a high rate of speed and all of the players within the health care supply chain, with the exception of employers, have shown themselves to be adept at embracing change. If employers aggressively get into the game, the other players will have to evolve or risk being left behind. There has been and there will continue to be resistance to change in the way employer-sponsored health insurance operates, but that should only reinforce the need to push ahead because the only group it isn't working for is employers.

At the time of this writing, there is a significant debate going on across the country as to the need for tariffs to put the US steel and aluminum industries on a level footing with producers from other countries. Students of the steel industry will know that it wasn't unfair trade practices that put the US steel industry on the brink of extinction, but rather it was hubris and unwillingness to evolve that did so. While countries throughout Europe and Asia embraced new technology and production methods, the big three US producers rested on their laurels and doubled down on outdated technology, with one exception. Ken Iverson, the CEO of Nucor, the largest steel producer in the US today, built the first mill using the electric arc process in the US in 1969 and over the coming decades his company came to dominate the industry. When asked about protectionist trade practices related to his industry, Iverson had the following to say, *"Unless you're under intense competitive pressure and it becomes a question of the survival of the business to do it, you're just going to lapse back into your old ways. There's no other answer."*[37]

I believe those words are very much applicable to the health care supply chain as well. The major players are constantly responding to competitive pressure from their peers and other outside forces, which require them to respond by evolving. There has been no pressure, however, from employers to demand a change in pricing and funding, and until there is they are just going to lapse into their old ways.

---

[37] https://www.inc.com/magazine/19860401/895.html, accessed June 2018.

Appendix NextGen Benefits Mastermind Partners Member List

Cathy Aitken
Corporate Benefit Analysis
Nashville, TN

Felipe Barganier
GAB International LLC
Atlanta, GA

Murray Bass
Borden Insurance
Corpus Christi, TX

Gary Becker
Becker Benefits
Baltimore, MD

Paula Beersdorf
Sun Risk Management
St. Petersburg, FL

James Blachek
Benefits Group
Clarks Summit, PA

John Clay
Better Source Benefits
Somerset, KY

Ben Conner
Conner Insurance
Indianapolis, IN

Dan Cronin
CGI Business Solutions
Hooksett, NH

Allison DePaoli
DePaoli Professional Services
San Antonio, TX

Kim Eckelbarger
Tropical Risk Management
Trinity, FL

Jeff Fox
HJ Spier
Indianapolis, IN

Bob Gearhart, Jr.
DCW Group
Boardman, OH

Bob Gearhart, Sr.
DCW Group
Boardman, OH

Randy Hansen
PSG Washington
Everett, WA

John Harris
CU Benefits
Beaverton, OR

Jeff Haudenschield
Benefits Group
Clarks Summit, PA

March Heath
InoVentive Solutions
Bremen, GA

Mike Hill
Coldbrook Insurance
Grand Rapids, MI

Lambert Hsu
BenefitPro
San Diego, CA

Todd Hudson
Hudson Planning Group
Wilmington, DE

Bill Hughes
Hughes Benefits
Waco, TX

Beth Johnson
Mitchell Insurance
Sikeston, MO

Mark Krogulski
E3 Strategy
Raleigh, NC

Craig Lack
ENERGI
San Juan Capistrano, CA

Deke Lape
Mitchell Insurance
Sikeston, MO

Kevin Lewis
Tailor-Made Benefits
Waco, TX

Michael Lutz
Compass Benefits Group
Brighton, MI

Andy Neary
Olson Group
Ft. Collins, CO

Tim Olson
Olson Group
Omaha, NE

Stefanie Pigeon
Affiliated Associates
Essex, VT

Karin Rettger
Principal Resource Group
Glen Ellyn, IL

Derek Rine
David Rine Insurance
Fairlawn, OH

Mick Rodgers
Axial Benefits Group
Burlington, MA

John Sbrocco
Questige Consulting
Madison, NJ

Dawn Sheue
Summit Insurance Services
Jackson, WY

Eric Silverman
Silverman Benefits
Towson, MD

Robert Slayton
Robert Slayton & Associates
Naperville, IL

Mark Snider
Snider, Fuller and Stroh
Athens, OH

Tom Stautberg
Stautberg Benefit Advisors
Cincinnati, OH

Trey Taylor
Taylor Insurance Services
Valdosta, GA

Dan Thompson
Gulfshore Insurance
Naples, FL

Brian Tolbert
Bernard Health
Nashville, TN

Nolan Waterfall
Qandun Insurance
Glendale, CA